1

**"Saw-whet Owl"**
© 1997 by David B. Johnson
sculpture - (10"x5"x5")
acrylic/gouache on wood
collection of the artist

Frontispiece:

**"The Noble" - Barn Owl**
© 1991 by Arnold Nogy
(25"x19")
transparent watercolor on Arches watercolor paper
* private collection

# Jeffrey Whiting's OWLS

## OF NORTH AMERICA

The Heliconia Press, Inc.
Clayton, Ontario

**"Prairie Cradle"**
© 1987 by Michael Dumas
(18"x18")
egg tempera on (rag) panel
*private collection

4

*Dedicated to my Grandmother, Phyllis Falconer.*

# Acknowledgments

First and foremost, my parents, Bill and Diane Whiting and grandmother, Phyllis Falconer, whose love, support, guidance and hard work have made this project possible. All have invested a great deal time, effort and money. A million thanks to Dr. Donald Smith of Carleton University for his support and provision of specimens from the university collection. Aleta Karstad contributed an heroic amount of time, effort and enthousiasm in helping to finish the painted illustrations and caligraphy. David Schincariol and Tina Mohns generously gave their time, skill and patience to this project. Dr. Fred Schueler was extremely helpful with editorial advice. Thanks to Perry and Pat McGregor for their selfless and crucial help in a time of great need. David Johnson's brain and friendship were indescribably helpful. Thanks to David Whiting for providing much needed guidance in my quest for western owls, and Maryanne, Emily and Brendan for their cheer and wonderful hospitality. Thanks to Chris Whiting for smoothing yet another leg of my journey and opening my eyes to the beauty of the Gulf Islands. Bill Kraft was extremely helpful and interested in providing a guided tour of the captive owls of Springwater Provincial Park as were Bill Gilroy of the Kamloops Wildlife Park and Richard Howie of the Ministry of Natural Resources, Kamloops, British Columbia. Monica Tolksdorf of Monica's Wildlife Shelter in Surrey, B.C. and Kathy Nihei of Nepean, Ontario's Wild Bird Care Center were kind enough allow the photographing of recovering captive birds. Special thanks to Kai Ansari for his patience, interest and determination to do business as well as Bernie Steele, Tom Lillico, James Blackler and the rest of the staff at Gilmore Print Services. In Saskatoon, Cam Merkle's hospitality, friendliness and guidance was greatly appreciated. Thanks to the Leigh Yawkey Woodson Art Museum for opening a new world of nature art and artists to me. Sina Mardani provided friendship and intelligent input as did Chris and Jen Whiting in brainstorming sessions. Thanks also to Michael Runtz, Ernie Sparks of Sparks Studios in Kingston Ontario, Ken and Jason Whiting, Rod Duncan, Graham Forbes, Anastasia Karvounis, Lee Gagne, Nicole Zaharko, Yasaman Fazli, Leonard and Lorraine Lee of Lee Valley Tools, Inc., Luke Cuccia of Books Plus, Bruce Stackhouse of Wood'n'feathers Carving Supplies...

... and all the artists who had faith in my project.

Thanks.

Published by
The Heliconia Press, Inc.
P.O. Box 200, Clayton, Ontario
Canada, K0A 1P0

Printed and bound in Canada

**Canadian Cataloguing in Publication Data**

Whiting, Jeffrey, 1972
    Jeffrey Whiting's Owls of North America

(Whiting's Reference of Birds; 1)
ISBN 1-896980-10-4 (leather bound).
ISBN 1-896980-09-0 (bound)

1. Owls-North America. 2. Owls-North America-Identification. 3. Owls in art.

I. Title.
II. Series.

QL696.S8W451997    598".97"097    C97-900036-X

10 9 8 7 6 5 4 3 2 1

First Edition
Whiting's Reference of Birds Series: ISBN 1-896980-00-7

Opposite:

**"Great Horned Owl"**
© 1985 by Rod Frederick
(26"x4")
oil on Belgian linen
*private collection

# Table of Contents

**"Immature Screech Owl"**
©1988 by Edward Aldrich
(15"x28")
oil on masonite
private collection

# Foreword By Michael Runtz

Owl. Few bird names conjure up such an identifiable image. Mention kinglet or vireo to a non-birder. Odds are nothing except a blank stare will come back your way. But OWL, well that's different. From preschoolers to senior citizens, everyone seems to share some intimacy with these birds even though they may never actually have seen one.

I became turned on to owls at a very early age. A young friend made me green with envy when he declared he had seen an OWL on the way to Sunday school! We both ended up skipping church to look for the bird but to my disappointment did not find it. To add insult to injury, my parents didn't sympathize when they learned I had sacrificed religion for a religious experience!

I finally met my first owl later that summer when a Great Horned Owl flushed from a towering pine, a murder of crows hot on its heels. But an even greater thrill came a year later on a Christmas Bird Count. A great commotion drew my attention to a large cedar grove. When I peered into the tree in which dozens of agitated chickadees were concentrated, I was ecstatic to find the centre of all the attention, a tiny Northern Saw-whet Owl!

Fortunately for me, I live in a part of Ontario where periodic incursions of northern owls occur. Some years as many as a dozen Great Grays or half a dozen Northern Hawk Owls can be seen within a thirty minute drive of my house. As I write this intro, we are in the midst of the biggest invasion of Boreal Owls ever. Four have turned up here, one appearing regularly at a friend's feeder. It has been great fun to watch this rare visitor roosting in a big pine during the day, ignoring the daily noisy inspections by all other birds.

All through recorded history owls have been revered and have been placed on a pedestal shared by few other birds. This infatuation is partly due to their mysterious ways. Owls are nocturnal hunters and their comings and goings are done in silence. That is unless they want to be heard. The booming territorial and courtship hoots of Great Horned and Barred Owls are quintessential components of the night mystique. No mystery or horror movie worth its salt fails to peak the tension with the mystical calls of one of these owls.

We are also intrigued with owls for their appearances. Huge eyes set in a big flat face give these birds a human-like appearance and a wise one at that. But even when the veil of mystery is lifted by scientific scrutiny, owls continue to captivate. Their acute hearing, derived partly from their peculiar facial configuration that captures and directs sound, allows owls to pinpoint prey in near-total darkness. An owl's trademark silent flight is afforded by large soft-edged feathers and huge wings. A special comb on the leading primary breaks up the air flowing over the wing, eliminating any sound that might alert a sharp-eared mouse to the hunter's approach. Owls can peer through the darkest of nights thanks to oversized eyes packed with light-sensitive rods. A reversible outer toe makes sure elusive prey doesn't slip away. Small prey is swallowed whole, the indigestible bones and fur later coughed out in neat balls known as pellets. Endowed with these sophisticated tools, owls are unrivalled hunters of darkness.

Whether you are an artist or just an owl fancier like me, Jeff Whiting's book will be a perfect addition to your library. Replete with the superb artwork of Jeff and a number of other extremely talented artists, this book is sure to become a classic reference. It will also play an important role in further immortalizing these intriguing creatures of the night.

Michael Runtz

Michael Runtz is a renowned naturalist/educator/photographer and the author of several bestselling nature books *Moose Country, Algonquin Seasons, The Explorer's Guide to Algonquin Park, Wild Flowers, Wild Things, and Wild Wings.* He resides in Arnprior, Ontario.

**"Shadows of Dusk" - Great Gray Owls**
© 1985 by Rod Frederick
(17"x35")
oil on Belgian linen
*private collection

# Introduction

ne might ask why this book exists, in particular among so many books available on birds in the marketplace today. This book's concept grew from the initial intent to provide two dimensional artists and particularly wildfowl carvers with a master reference to the external anatomy for North American owls, to the same degree as the earlier *Common Loon - an anatomical portfolio for the wildlife artist* did for the Common Loon. My approach was to illustrate as completely and systemmatically as I could. I worked from specimens and photographs as if I would never have access to them again and these illustrations would be all I would ever have to work from in the future. While I examined this niche, I realized that there is a much broader audience interested in the illustrations I was creating. It is my hope to provide the owner of this book with the next best thing to a bird in the hand - live, study skin or otherwise. *Jeffrey Whiting's Owls of North America* is the first in a long string of special books whose intent is to provide the bird enthusiast with a comprehensive visual master reference to the birds of North America in an aesthetic format. I do not pretend to describe this book as a master reference in written material, although I have tried to systemmatically include all information that I believe is of most interest to serious birders, about the life histories of the nineteen species. There are no new concepts described within the text of this book, and the information that is present has been carefully selected from various publications and treatises listed in the recommended reading section at the end of the book. My books are intended to be the next logical informational step beyond the field guide.

The technical profiles or multi-view ink studies are designed to be used directly as reference patterns for carvers, while the color study plates can be referred to for feather count, shape, color and identification. The color plates in the species profile section were created to provide the viewer with the next best thing to a study skin. In many ways I believe these studies to be much better than a skin for the purposes of most people, in that I have done a lot of work in counting and organizing the otherwise intermingled, or partially moulted feather tracts. In creating these "anatomical templates", the specimens were neither traced nor transferred directly from photograph. Instead each bird has been reconstructed from the "bones up" - literally, referring not only to a single shrunken and mothballed specimen, but as well, frozen (thawed actually) specimens (both provided graciously by Carleton University's zoological collection and the Royal Ontario Museum) and a plethora of photographs. Not only have an untold number of books and colorful periodicals been desecrated but I spent six weeks travelling across the continent, photographing and observing live, captive birds at zoos and rehabilitation centers. Perhaps they themselves might have ended up published if I were not such an abominable photographer.

Artists in particular might be interested to hear that I was able to paint all species of owls exclusively, with the exception of some eyes, with the four earth tones, Raw Umber, Raw Sienna, Burnt Sienna and Burnt Umber, plus black and white and occasionally Yellow Ochre. What this suggests to artists is, mixing paints should be quite straightforward, and for those not interested in painting, all species of North American owls are colored to be as invisible as possible, or cryptic, to use the proper terminology.

The artwork presented in this book requires special attention. I am most gratified by the tremendous response of artists whom I specifically invited to contribute their work. Over a third of those asked, submitted work. I boldly asked artist colleagues of diverse media, many of world renown, most of whom I have yet to meet, and all of highest credentials and talent, to have faith and contribute work to the project of an individual with limited track record. I am confident that none will regret having participated. The artwork concept grew from the acceptance that I was not a capable photographer, and from the realization that this book's audience would appreciate the beauty of subject-specific paintings and sculpture over yet more photographs. As an artist focussing on natural subject matter, I also saw this as a chance to showcase the talent of artists painting and sculpting in my scene, perhaps lending a little more credibility to an otherwise underrated area of visual arts - nature art.

This book has evolved greatly and in several small circles since its conceptual genesis. Enjoy this one, then keep your eyes peeled. There are more on the way.

# Gallery of Owl Art

**"Out on a Limb" - Northern Hawk Owl**
© 1988 Karen L. Allaben-Confer
(17"x21")
pencil and pastel on white Stonehenge etching paper
collection of Phyllis and Gene Likens

**"Windfall" - Saw-whet Owl**
© 1988 Karen L. Allaben-Confer
(38"x24")
pencil and pastel on white Stonehenge etching paper
collection of Phyllis and Gene Likens

Opposite:

**"Winter Wind" - Barred Owl**
©1992 by Edward Aldrich
(34"x36")
oil on masonite
private collection

**"Patience" - Great Horned Owl**
© 1990 by Charles Allmond
sculpture - (18.5"x11"x4.5")
Utah alabaster on teakwood base
*collection of the artist

**"Saw-whet Brooding"**
© 1980 by Tony Angell
sculpture-(4.5"x5"x6")
serpentine
private collection

**"The Hunter"** - Short-eared Owl
© 1993 by Brian Arneill
(14.5"x21")
watercolor with body color on Saunders Waterford paper
collection of Mr. and Mrs C. Cathcart

Opposite:

**"Great Horned Owl"**
© 1995 by Barbara Banthien
(13"x9")
gouache on 100% rag Bristol board
collection of the artist

**"Winter Spirit" - Snowy Owl**
© 1992 by Alan Barnard
(19"x29")
pencil crayons and gouache
private collection

**"Capture" - Great Horned Owl**
© 1989 by Clarence Cameron
sculpture - (9"x9"x9")
dendritic soapstone
collection of the artist

**"Barn Owl"**
© 1990 by Clarence Cameron
sculpture - (7"x5"x6")
dendritic soapstone
collection of the artist

**"The Last Leaves of Autumn"** - Saw-whet Owl
© 1983 by Michael Dumas
(20"x28")
watercolor and gouache on cotton rag board
*private collection

**"Idle Threat" - Great Horned
Owl and Douglas Squirrel**
© 1994 by Kathleen E. Dunn
(12"x22")
oil on masonite
private collection

**"Observation Point"** - **Eastern Screech Owl**
© 1993 by Gary Eigenberger
sculpture - (24"x6.5"x10.5")
oil on basswood
private collection

**"Nightwings" - Barred Owl**
© 1992 by Beth Erlund
(16"x22")
batik on cotton
*collection of the artist

**"Do Not Disturb" - Barn Owl**
© 1991 by Beth Erlund
(18"x22")
batik on cotton
*collection of the artist

**"After the Storm"** - **Short-eared Owl**
© 1986 by Barry C. Flahey
(21"x30")
transparent watercolor
*collection of the artist

**"In the Lee of the Elm" - Great Gray Owl**
© 1996 by Barry C. Flahey
(21.5"x30")
transparent watercolor
collection of the artist

**"Autumn Leaves (detail)"** - Spotted Owl
© 1989 by Rod Frederick
(29"x9")
oil on Belgian linen
* private collection

**"Silent Watch" - Great Horned Owl**
© 1989 by Rod Fredrick
(18"x16")
oil on Belgian linen
* private collection

**"Barn Owl"**
© 1994 by Andrew Hutchinson
(21"x15.5")
gouache on Frisk CS2 hot press watercolor board
* private collection

**"Great Horned Owl"**
© 1981 by Cary Hunkel
(24"x18")
charcoal and colored pencils on charcoal paper
private collection

**"Snowy Owl"**
© 1995 by M.C. Kanouse
(20"x14")
transparent watercolor on Arches 300 lb CP
collection of the artist

Opposite:

**"Eastern Screech Owl"**
© 1994 by Aleta Karstad
(15"x11")
transparent watercolor
private collection

**"In the Morning Frost"** - Great Horned Owl
© 1988 by Michael Klafke
(24"x36")
oil on masonite
collection of the artist

**"Summer Watch" - Barn Owl**
© 1982 by Stephen Lyman
(26"x50")
acrylic on board
private collection

**"A Closer Look" - Barred Owl**
© 1995 by Cindy Markowski
(20"x16")
acrylic on masonite
collection of the artist

**"Nobody's Angel"**
© 1991 by Walter T. Matia
sculpture - (14"x11"x10")
bronze on granite
*collection of the artist

**"Narrow Escape" - Snowy Owl**
© 1993 by Arnold Nogy
(20.25"x29")
transparent watercolor on Arches watercolor paper
* private collection

**"Uncertain Outlook" - Barn Owl**
© 1993 by Jeremy Paul
(15"x22")
acrylic on Bockingford paper
* private collection

**"Scots Pine" - Long-eared Owl**
© 1993 by Jeremy Paul
(22"x12")
acrylic on Bockingford paper
private collection

**"White Pine Vigil- Barred Owl"**
© by Jeremy Pearse
(30"x40")
oil on canvas
private collection

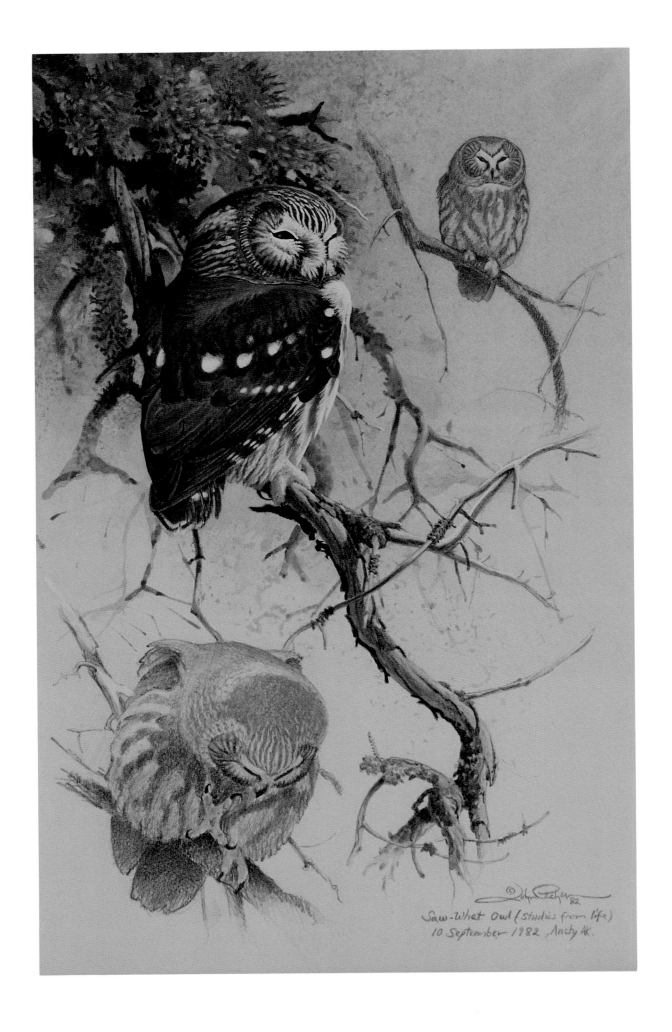

Saw-Whet Owl (Studies from life)
10 September 1982, Anch, Ak.

Opposite:

**"Saw-whet Owl Studies"**
© 1982 by John Charles Pitcher
(15"x9.5")
watercolor and pencil on watercolor board
private collection

**"Burrowing Owls"**
© 1987 by Andrea Rich
(12.5"x12.5")
woodcut on Koyo paper
* collection of the artist

**"Alaskan Cotton" - Snowy Owl**
© 1995 by Sueellen Ross
(27.5"x23")
mixed: India ink, watercolor and colored pencil on
Arches 140 lb. hot pressed paper
private collection

**"Perched in the Fir" - Boreal Owl**
© 1992 by Joan Sharrock
(18"x14")
oil on linen canvas
collection of the artist

**"Barred Owl"**
© 1995 by John Sill
(13.5"x10.5")
transparent watercolor on Arches rough 300 lb.
collection of the artist

**"Great Horned Owls"**
© 1995 by John Soulliere
(36"x30")
batik on hand-woven silk
collection of the artist

**"Short-eared Owl"**
© 1993 by Haruo Uchiyama
sculpture - (28"x12"x12")
acrylic on wood

Opposite:

**"Snowy Owl and Crows"**
© 1992 by Gijsbert van Frankenhuyzen
(28"x22")
acrylic on canvas
private collection

**"Great Horned Owl"**
© 1989 by Gijsbert van Frankenhuyzen
(22"x28")
acrylic on canvas
collection of the artist

**"Night Tiger" - Great Horned Owl**
© 1995 by Paula G. Waterman
(23"x19")
scratchboard on British Scraperboard
collection of Francisco Diaz and Molly Saudidge

**"Saw-whet in Jackpine"**
© 1995 by Jeffrey Whiting
sculpture - (16"x20"x14")
acrylic on metal & tupelo/ oil on maple and bamboo
collection of the artist

**"Great Horned Owl"**
© 1990 by Jeffrey Whiting
sculpture - (16"x10"x8")
oil on tupelo
private collection

# Owls at a Glance

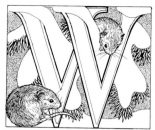hile many types of birds have been popularized from the recent boom in birding, none, save perhaps the Common Loon, evoke the emotional response that owls do. Throughout history and no doubt human prehistory, owls have figured prominently in virtually every culture. They have been feared as well as revered, but in all cases they commanded a great deal of respect. In ancient Greece the owl accompanied the powerful Goddess of Wisdom, Athena. The owl was seen, the world over, as a harbinger of death. In either case, its mysterious nocturnal habit, hair-raising calls, seemingly unnatural tameness and human-like facial qualities have inspired countless myths, legends and cosmic interpretations.

Although it is still unclear what defines a true owl from an ancestral relative, we know now that easily recognizable owls appeared shortly after the demise of the dinosaurs. The oldest known owl, at present, is *Ogygoptynx wetmorei*. Its fossil remains were unearthed in 1916 and date back to the Paleocene Epoch, almost 65 million years ago. The earliest examples of tytonid owls date back to the Eocene, around 53 to 54 million years ago. Two genera are currently recognized: *Eostrix* and *Minerva*. Familiar genera such as *Bubo, Otus* and *Strix* appeared at approximately the same time that hominids did, around 26 million years ago in the Miocene. By the Pleistocene, in coexistence with modern humans, owls reached a peak in diversity.

Often, until recently, Strigiformes, or the taxonomical group which describes Owls, were closely associated in non-scientific literature with other large predatory birds such as hawks, falcons and eagles under a collective term 'Birds of Prey'. This was an artificial and misleading classification. Taxonomists have always agreed that the similarities which exist between these aerial hunters are the direct result of a process called evolutionary convergence, whereby two distantly related organisms evolve similar characteristics when occupying the same ecological niche. While they do share a common avian ancestor, they also share this lineage with a wide range of other distantly related birds of much less surficial similarity such as hummingbirds and kingfishers. The talons, sharp bill and predaceous habits are all solutions to survival adopted independently by each group through independent systems of natural selection. In the popular literature of recent years, owls have been properly associated with cuckoos, frogmouths, nightjars and parrots. Recent work on DNA comparisons have only confirmed these relationships. The following is a current taxonomic description of the two families of owls, Tytonidae and Strigidae...

Kingdom: Animalia
Phylum: Chordata
Subphylum: Vertebrata
Class: Aves (Birds)
Order: Strigiformes (Owls)
Family: Tytonidae (Monkey-faced Owls); Strigidae (True Owls)
Genus: eg. Tyto
Species: eg. alba
Subspecies: eg. alba

The essence of an owl is an amazing combination of unique and highly adapted characteristics. Its voice, coloration, feather structure and audio/visual skills are each, on their own, diagnostic of the group of birds we call owls.

The voice of an owl has always contributed in no small way to its reputation as a spook of the night. All species have several different vocalizations. The Great Horned Owl and Great Gray Owl both produce very deep, sonorous hoots. Screech owls produce an eerie winnowing sound. Most species occasionally utter blood-curdling screeches. The Barn Owl is a master of producing frightening hisses and screams. This, combined with its habit of taking up residence in abandoned homes and churches and its ghostly pale coloration, no doubt adds to the haunting imagery.

Owls exhibit a type of sexual dimorphism omnipresent in other birds of prey. Females tend to be significantly larger than males. In terms of coloration and feather patterns, male and female owls are virtually indistinguishable.

Intricate cryptic patterns abound on owls. This feature became very obvious to me while painting them. Aside from the eyes and feet, I found I could accurately paint them while limiting myself to earth tones alone plus black and white. Aside from eye and bill coloration, the color of all species of owls can be described in terms of light and dark values of the four earth tones (standard painting colors): burnt umber (dark red-brown), burnt sienna (red-brown), raw umber (dark yellow-brown) and raw sienna (yellow-brown) plus occasionally an earthy yellow (yellow ochre). Superficially, the markings on the most cryptic and mottled species such as the Eastern and Western Screech, Long-eared, and Great Horned Owl, appear random from feather to feather. Following a specific tract, feather by feather, from one end of the tract to the other, will reveal a subtle evolution of organized patterns.

In general, an owl's feathers are soft and fluffy. Close examination shows how extraordinarily airy and soft the body feathers really are. One can practically bury one's hands from sight in the mane of a Great Gray Owl.

Conversely, the feathers of a penguin are as stiff as scales. Both types of feathers, however, share the same basic structure. Feather structure consists of a central stiff shaft or rachis. Numerous parallel strands called barbs extend from both sides of this shaft approximately 60° from perpendicular. Along each of these barbs, numerous tiny hook-like structures called barbules or hamuli are usually present. These facing rows of barbules shape the feather by holding the barbs together and when detached, appear as a feather split. In owls, much of their plumage lacks effective barbules, so barbs remain independent and hair-like.

The wing of a bird is a remarkable structure. Unlike the wings of a bat or a pterosaur, which are vulnerable to a single debilitating tear, those of a bird are fundamentally resilient to damage since the entire flying structure is compartmentalized into rows of flight feathers, each of which is replaced during moult. There are five distinct types of flight feathers: (1) the rectrices or tail feathers; (2) the primary flight feathers, defined by their direct attachment to the metacarpal (hand plus fused digits; owls have 10 primaries); (3) the secondary flight feathers, defined by their direct attachment to the forearm; (4) the tertial flight feathers, defined by their direct attachment to the humerus; and (5) the ulula, effectively an extension of the thumb on the leading edge of the wing, used to varying degrees in different flying situations.

Stiff flight feathers such as primaries, secondaries and rectrices require rigidity and so are heavily shafted and barbuled. One thing that makes owls unique among birds in this respect is the apparent exception to this general rule. The very edges and ends of the flight feathers are frayed while the interior of these feathers is tightly bound by barbules. The result is a "rough" edge which induces a small amount of turbulence where the wings slice through the air in flight. That turbulence, when combined with the owl's naturally billowy-soft coverts, has a muffling effect and allows the birds to fly completely silently. The advantage to silence in flight is obvious for a predator which relies largely on surprise to catch its prey. All North American species except the Elf Owl share this quality. Strix owls and screech owls seem to have the most heavily fringed flight feathers while those of the Northern Hawk, Burrowing, Northern and Ferruginous Pygmy and Snowy Owls are more saw-toothed than fringed.

Owls feed largely on small rodents such as mice and voles. Small birds are also common prey and to a lesser extent, insects and other arthropods and occassionally small amphibians and reptiles. Some of the larger species of owls will also not hesitate to capture and devour smaller owls. Great Horned Owls are known to kill house cats, and perhaps more amazingly, Striped Skunks. As an order, owls are diverse feeders; however some, such as the Snowy Owl, rely on only a small number of prey species for sustenance.

Owls characteristically perch with two toes directed forward and two opposing ones behind. Most birds have a three-forward, one back configuration. The most important function of this morphology is the improved grasping ability during hunting. Interestingly, owls prefer to carry prey on the wing in their bills rather than in their talons. Typically, owl talons are needle-sharp and sharply curved. The Flammulated Owl, which feeds entirely on insects, is an exception, with relatively weak feet and reduced talons. Barn Owls have a comb-like ridge along the edges of their talons. This is a specialized structure used in grooming and parasite removal. Similar structures appear on some wading birds.

Most owls hunt from a perch, relying on their night vision and sound cues. Prey is virtually always caught by a stealthy airborne approach ending in a quick grab and deathly bite on the ground. The victims are often caught largely, sometimes exclusively, by sound. An amazing example of this is the Great Gray Owl's blind plunge through many inches of snow (even with a crust) onto a completely unsuspecting rodent, with a very high success rate. Some species, such as the Great Horned, Boreal and Northern Saw-whet Owl practise food caching, that is, they will kill a prey item and hide it in a secure spot. Taking advantage of low winter temperatures, they will return to their frozen food source, perching on it to thaw it out before eating.

Owls generally swallow their prey whole. As a result of this practice, a lot of indigestible material, such as bone and hair, is also ingested. Instead of passing this waste entirely through the gut, owls have adopted an interesting technique, shared with hawks, grebes, herons and ravens, of disposing of this waste in the form of a regurgitated pellet. The swallowed prey is broken down in the ventriculus, a glandular pouch early in the digestive tract. Here enzymes liquify the soft nutritious parts of the food. This liquid then passes further along the digestive tract. The remaining hair, feathers, teeth, bone or hardened insect parts are compacted into a tight elongate ball which is subsequently coughed up. The discharged pellet is remarkably dry and is very useful to researchers. Often intact skulls of deceased rodents or other prey are present, making identification quite straightforward. Areas of pellet accumulation are also excellent indicators of roosting spots of owls.

One of the attributes that endears owls to humans is the same characteristic which makes them such lethal and enigmatic hunters. Their big, round and stereoscopic eyes give them a human, child-like quality. Their brows make these eyes even more expressive and lend personality. The eyes are oriented approximately 45° from forward, giving them around 90° of visual field overlap directly in front of them. This means they have depth perception within that range of overlap. Owls also commonly bob and swing their heads in an exaggerated motion. This exercise is performed to determine the position of objects by means of triangulation. Though some owls do hunt during the day, they all share the ability to see with apparent daylight clarity in the darkest of nights. Some are exclusively nocturnal hunters, such as the Eastern Screech and Barn Owls, while others are more crepuscular. All, however, are capable of seeing in daylight.

Owl eyes are tubular in shape. As with all birds, their eyes are unable to move freely within a socket and are supported and surrounded by bony sheaths called sclerotic rings. As a result, the owl must swing its entire head around to direct its vision. In fact, the necks of owls have adapted to be so flexible that they are able to turn nearly 270°. The tubular configuration allows the characteristically round lens to be placed relatively far from the equivalently rounded retina. The advantage of this shape lies in the ability to magnify an image with the abnormally rounded lens, without sacrificing light intensity reaching the retina.

Owls are color-blind. The reason for this is an evolutionary trade-off in favour of resolution over color definition. The eyes of owls share the same structures as humans. The basic design of the eye is the same. Two types of light receptor cells occur in the retina. One type, the rod cell, specializes in light intensity for shape definition. The other, the cone cell, is responsible for distinguishing color. While humans see in vibrant color and reasonable definition, owls see with telescopic clarity, but in shades of grey. This is because owls have a proportionally high count of rod cells over cone cells. In addition to this adaptation, the rod cells in owls contain a pigment called rhodopsin, otherwise known as "visual purple". This amazing chemical enhances shape interpretation of light, producing a definite image in the owl's brain, where we would interpret the signal as a general presence of a light source.

A tapetum lucidum, or "cateye" effect gives illuminated owl eyes their usually reddish, eerily reflected brilliance at night. This characteristic is an adaptation common among many nocturnal animals. Domestic cats are perhaps the best known example. In such creatures, light passes through the pupil to the receptor cells of the retina behind which the light is reflected back by the tapetum. As a result of the reflection, light passes back through the retina. The image is enhanced in two ways by this effect. Not only is the absolute quantity of light reaching the retina greater (by about 40%) but, the contrast between the subject being eyed and the background is increased.

If the visual capabilities of owls seem impressive, then their sense of hearing is truly awe-inspiring. Though there remains a bit of controversy over some of the mechanics involved, there is a clear consensus on the fact that owls hear extremely well. An owl can hunt on the basis of sound alone, making instantaneous adjustments to its course as it approaches its prey. More northerly species, which especially depend on hearing during the dark months when prey are largely concealed by snow cover, have an asymmetrical placement and shape of the ears. The Boreal Owl is a particularly extreme example of this adaptation. The mechanics of the asymmetrical configuration are not clearly understood. However they are almost certainly involved in the locating of a sound source in three-dimensional space. The ear openings of all owls are very large relative to the size of the skull and are broadly fringed with a feathered skin flap. The openings are hidden directly behind the facial discs. It is thought that the stiff feathered discs form parabolic dishes funnelling and amplifying sound directly to the ears. Upon determining the basic location of the source, the owl leaves its perch, flying silently toward its objective. It makes subtle, precise adjustments to its striking path right up until impact.

Ear tufts are prominent features on many species of owls and are small to absent on others. They are excellent field markers for species identification in that their presence or absence can narrow the options for the birdwatcher. They perform no function for hearing but rather are an adaptation for camouflage, and serve to break up the owl's silhouette when raised.

Courtship in owls is complex and involves strong pair bonding rituals such as mutual grooming and preening, particularly in those species which mate for life. Early stages of courtship include presentation of food gifts by the male to the female. Male Great Horned Owls perform extravagant tail wagging, body-bobbing, throat patch expanding and utter loud cries. Breeding and incubation times vary from species to species and population to population due to climatic differences. Great Horned Owls will begin breeding season as early as New Year's Day in the warmest parts of their range. Incubation lasts around a month for most owls and fledging time will take anywhere from four weeks to two months.

Most owls are largely sedentary. Migrations are usually either roaming movement of individuals or punctuated events of mass movement of species members in a southerly direction in years of food scarcity. The result is the appearance of great numbers of Snowy, Great Gray, Boreal, and Northern Hawk Owls every few years, as far south as the northern United States. Some species do migrate, however, in the purer sense of the word. The northern populations of Short-eared, Long-eared, Elf and

Northern Saw-whet Owls migrate south during winter. Long-ears will winter as far south as Mexico, while the others will move southward within Canada and the United States. Not much is known about the exact movement of the Elf Owls but they seem to vanish from the northern parts of their breeding range between early fall and spring.

If threatened, owls will either attempt to be as inconspicuous as possible, relying on their cryptic coloration for invisibility, or adopt a menacing defensive pose. Their reaction depends largely on whether or not they are nesting or brooding. If there are eggs or young to defend, most species are fearless and ferocious defenders. The feet and talons rather than the bill are used in defence and combat. Otherwise, many species of owls appear tame to the point of foolishness. In fact, smaller species such as the Northern Saw-whet Owl will not only allow themselves to be approached, but even to be picked up by a curious human observer.

Common, but less openly aggressive than an all-out attack in reaction to a potential danger, is a threat display. Young will hiss and clack their bills. Bill clacking is practiced by owls young and old, but less experienced owls have a less refined method of achieving the clacking sound. Young will snap their bills together and quickly retract their tongues to produce the clack. They may do this long enough and hard enough to draw blood from their tongues if the perceived threat persists. More experienced bill-clackers keep the tongue out of the way, rapidly closing their bills and shifting their position so they snap together more completely. Long-eared Owls tilt their wings upwards and fan them in an attempt to intimidate a threat by their newly imposing size.

Owls most commonly nest in tree cavities and vacant corvid or raptor nests. Elf Owls usually nest in woodpecker nest holes in saguaro cacti. Snowy Owls nest on the ground. Burrowing Owls nest underground. Barn Owls have a great affinity for civilization, nesting in vacant buildings and farm equipment. Only Barn Owls seem to have successfully taken to human-made nest boxes. Owls have only one brood per year. Young owls are born in an altricial state, that is to say, in a helpless, totally dependent, nestbound form. They hatch with their eyes closed and are covered in white down.

Owls continue to fascinate humans, even though much of their supernatural reputation has given way in large part to biological understanding. They command a new kind of respect with their highly specialized habits and adaptations. Each species reveals its own characteristic wonders too... but that is the next chapter.

# Templates of External Anatomy and Species Descriptions

# Barn Owl

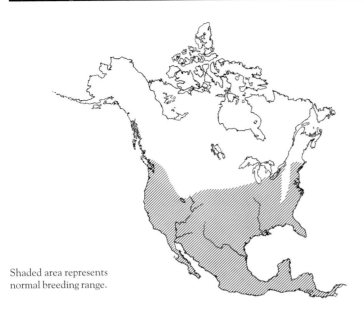

Shaded area represents normal breeding range.

| STATISTICS | |
|---|---|
| STATUS: | locally threatened |
| LENGTH: | 35.5-51 cm. (14-20 in.) |
| WINGSPAN: | 1.1-1.2m. (43-47 in.) |
| MASS: | male avg. .44 kg. (16oz); |
| | female avg. .49 kg. (17oz.) |
| LIFESPAN: | up to 17 yrs. |
| CLUTCH SIZE: | 3-11 |
| EGGS: | white to off-white; elliptical; |
| | ~43 x 33mm. (~1.7 x 1.3 in.) |
| INCUBATION: | 32-34 days |
| FLEDGING: | 52-56 days |

The Barn Owl is a medium-sized, earless, slender owl and the only member of the Monkey-faced Owl family (Tytonidae) in North America. Its wings are long and pointed and extend beyond the tail when folded. Legs and tarsi are also elongated. The tarsi and toes are sparsely feathered to bare, with long, sharp claws. It has a heart-shaped, pale face with dark umber eyes and a straw-colored bill. The Barn Owl is quite pale relative to most other owls. It seems likely that its ghostly white silhouette combined with its eerie voice and habit of occupying deserted buildings gave rise to many haunted house myths.

The Barn Owl is a nocturnal predator, which has few natural enemies in the Americas. Great Horned Owls are its greatest threat. If bothered it will adopt exaggerated antagonistic postures which incorporate head bobbing, shaking and swaying, hissing, foot stomping and an impressive display of inflated feathers. Attacks on humans, in defence of the nest, are rare. When roosting, the owl adopts a strange position, in which the otherwise rounded facial discs are contracted into narrow slits with the folded wings tucked tightly into the body. Hunting generally occurs on the wing over clearings and marshy areas.

### OTHER ENGLISH NAMES
American barn owl; monkey-faced owl, church owl, golden owl; stone owl; white owl; white-breasted barn owl

### DIMORPHISM
Females are slightly darker, more boldly marked and, slightly larger on average (~11%).

### DISTRIBUTION
The species *Tyto alba* is found on all continents except Antarctica. In North America, it is confined largely south of the Canadian border, except in extreme southwestern British Columbia and extreme southern Ontario.

### HABITAT
The Barn Owl is found in all climatic zones except the tundra and boreal forest. It is generally limited to areas below 250 m (750 ft.) above sea level. Barn Owls tend to prefer arid areas to humid ones and are often associated with fields and grasslands and at the edge of forests. Human-built structures seem to provide Barn Owls with their preferred roosting and nesting spots. Such structures include barns, church towers, attics, lofts, sheds, cisterns, mine shafts and almost any other vacant build-

ing or sheltered space. Other more wild places for daytime roosting include sheltered rocky ledges, cracks, holes, caves and dense foliage in heavily wooded areas.

### SUBSPECIES
Only one subspecies has been described for the Americas- *T. alba pratincola*. It is also the largest race among up to 40 subspecies worldwide.

### VOICE
Barn Owls have a wide variety of voices. Unlike many of their strigid cousins, they do not produce deep, sonorous hoots. Instead their vocal repertoire consists of catlike hissing, screeching, tongue-clicking, rasping screeches and purring. Their territorial call is a loud hissing scream. Begging young hiss.

### BREEDING HABITS
Barn Owls will nest in almost any type of hole, but particularly in dark recesses of human-made structures or ruins such as church towers, attics, barns, haystacks, deep wells, large wooden nest boxes (preferably within barns), and abandoned agricultural machinery. Other nesting sites include tall trees such as cottonwoods and palms. Though generally territorial, successful nests have been

found within a few metres of each other.

Breeding occurs almost year-round. Eggs are usually laid from March to June. Clutch size is highly variable (from 3 to 11) with an average of 5 to 6, and eggs are laid in 1 to 2-day intervals. The female alone incubates for 32-34 days while the male hunts and performs guard duty. The female will begin hunting after the youngest chick reaches two weeks of age. Perhaps oddly, young do not fight over food, but will even feed smaller, begging siblings, though unhealthy young may be cannibalized. Fledging occurs after 52-56 days.

## MIGRATION

Those dwelling in the northernmost areas of their range commonly move southward in winter.

## PREY

The Barn Owl has a specialized diet. About 95% consists of small rodents, particularly voles, followed by mice and shrews. Birds make the remainder along with occasional reptiles, amphibians, bats and arthropods.

JW '97
½-SIZE
BARN OWL

# Barn Owl

Scale: 40%

# Flammulated Owl

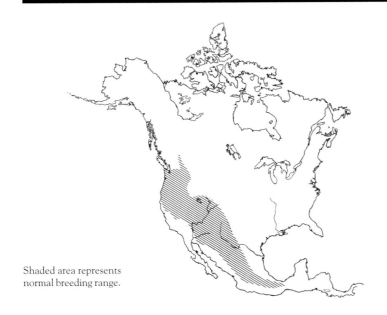

Shaded area represents
normal breeding range.

STATISTICS
STATUS:        uncommon
LENGTH:        15-18 cm. (6-7 in.)
WINGSPAN:      36-48 cm. (14-19 in.)
MASS:          male avg. 54 gm.;
               female avg. 57 gm.; 2oz.
CLUTCH:        2-4
EGGS:          white; oval ;
               ~29 x 25.5 mm. (1.1 x 1 in.)
INCUBATION:    unknown
FLEDGING:      unknown

The Flammulated Owl is North America's smallest "eared" owl. Its size, reclusiveness and limited range have left it largely unstudied. It has dark brown eyes and relatively small ear tufts. Its tail is relatively short, it has more pointed wings than the screech owls and its toes are unfeathered. The face is mottled grey/brown with some rufous leading up to ear tufts. Brows are white. Grey/brown with limited rufous mottling/vermiculation with dark central streaking is found on the crown, nape, cape, scapular, wing coverts, back and rump feathers. The white spots on the outermost scapular feathers are heavily edged in burnt sienna. Flight feathers are similarly colored, but barred. Underside, chest, belly and side feathers are much lighter and boldly marked.

### OTHER ENGLISH NAMES
Flammulated screech owl

### DIMORPHISM
Females, on average, are dimensionally slightly larger and heavier than males.

### DISTRIBUTION
Flammulated Owls live and breed in the pine forests of western North American mountains. At the northern extent of their range they are rare inhabitants of southern British Columbia. They range south through Idaho into the Rocky Mountains of Northern Colorado, through the Cascade Mountains and Sierra Nevada to southern California, Arizona, New Mexico, West Texas, and through the highlands of Mexico to Guatemala.

### HABITAT
Temperate to subtropical, dry, open mountain pine forests with shrubby understorey constitute most of the Flammulated Owls' habitat, where they inhabit primarily ponderosa pine, aspen and oak. They are generally restricted to elevations above 800 metres (2500 ft.) and can be found ranging as high up as 2700 metres (8300 ft.) in southern California and even higher in Mexico.

### SUBSPECIES
There is no consensus on the number of subspecies, if any. As many as six have been described.

### VOICE
The Flammulated Owl's territorial song is a surprisingly low-pitched soft hoot, alone or in pairs - *hoop* or *hoop-oop*, uttered at regular several-second intervals. When alarmed, its call is hoarser and includes barks and clucks. The female has a much higher-pitched call.

### BREEDING HABITS
Little is known of the Flammulated Owl's breeding and nesting habits. Some nests have been discovered in woodpecker nesting holes and some in nest boxes. They will lay between 2 and 4 eggs per clutch.

### MIGRATION
Little is known definitively about the Flammulated Owl's population dynamics. It has been long considered a migrant throughout its North American range, moving south for winter, but likely lives year-round on its breeding range in southern regions.

**PREY**

Winged insects compose virtually all of the Flammulated Owl's diet, and of these, moths, particularly noctuids, and butterflies predominate. Grasshoppers, crickets and other orthopterans are common meals as are many nocturnal insects. Other arthropods regularly taken include centipedes, millipedes, and various types of arachnids, including scorpions. Unlike most other owls, the Flammulated will often break up its prey prior to consuming it.

JW '97
FULL-SIZE
FLAMMULATED OWL

# Flammulated Owl

Scale: 100%

# Eastern Screech Owl

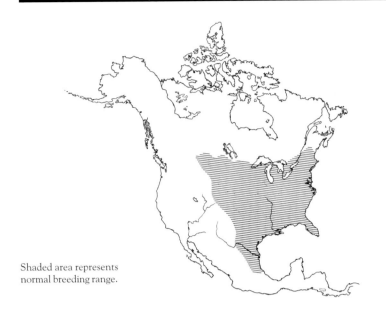

Shaded area represents
normal breeding range.

The Eastern and Western Screech Owls comprise a superspecies called the Common Screech Owl, distinguished from each other by their mutually exclusive geographical ranges. The Eastern Screech Owl is the only small owl in the east with ear tufts. There are two color morphs of the species (red and grey) which occur in both sexes. They have yellow eyes and their bills are light grey to straw. Their wings are quite rounded. The grey phase is a complex cryptic pattern of mottled brown and grey. The face is similarly mottled with faint radial light and dark banding around the eyes, with light brows. Superficially, the red phase is a more uniform color. The upper parts are almost exclusively, except for flight and tail feathers, a uniform sienna with dark central streaks on most feathers.

## OTHER ENGLISH NAMES
Scritch owl; grey owl; little duke owl; little cat owl; little horned owl; mottled owl; red owl; shivering owl; squinch owl; whickering owl.

## DIMORPHISM
The dimorphism that occurs in this species is not sexual. The red and grey color morphs occur in both sexes as do the less frequent intermediate phases.

## DISTRIBUTION
Breeds from southern Canadian prairie provinces through the great lakes region to southern Quebec and Maine, south continuously, east of the Rockies to northeast Mexico.

## HABITAT
Found widely in mixed and deciduous forests of eastern North America, from up to 1800 metres elevation in the Rocky Mountain foothills, and cottonwood groves of the prairies, to temperate mixed forests of the Great Lakes region, and subtropical forests of Florida to northeastern Mexico. They favour forest edges, gardens, orchards and other relatively open woodlands over dense bush.

## SUBSPECIES
The number of recognized Eastern Screech Owl subspecies is undetermined but ranges anywhere from zero to nine. Some commonly accepted races include the largest, *O. a. naevius*, from southern Ontario and *O. a. maxwelliae*, from the northwestern extent of their range, and the smallest from Florida, *O. a. floridanus*.

## VOICE
The Eastern Screech Owl's territorial call consists of a descending, tremulous wailing. The courtship call is a lone rolling trill or whinny of a constant pitch, often increasing in intensity toward the end. The female's call is of higher pitch. Occasionally bark-like whistles are uttered in alarm or sexual excitement.

## BREEDING HABITS
Cavities in trees and nestboxes, particularly old flicker holes, are the Eastern Screech Owl's preferred nesting sites. Due to its wide latitudinal range, breeding and incubating times vary from region to region; however, they are typically several weeks behind the Great Horned Owl. The female performs the incubating of 2 to 8 eggs, while the male hunts and provides food for her and the young. Incubation lasts 26 days, and young first leave the nest at 28 days.

## MIGRATION
Eastern Screech owls are strictly residential, living year round on their breeding ground.

# *Otus asio* (Linnaeus)

**PREY**

The Eastern Screech Owl enjoys a diverse diet of small mammals, birds, reptiles, amphibians and insects. Of the mammals, rats, mice, voles, bats and squirrels provide meals. Its diet also includes a wide variety of small bird prey, from warblers to pigeons. The Eastern Screech Owl also relies on frogs, snakes, newts, lizards, fish and a broad range of arthropods, including moths, beetles, arachnids, and crayfish.

JW '97
FULL-SIZE
EASTERN SCREECH OWL

# Eastern Screech Owl

**Note:** This plate shows only the red phase of the Eastern Screech Owl. See Western Screech Owl plate on pages 80/81 for grey phase

**Scale: 85%**

# Western Screech Owl

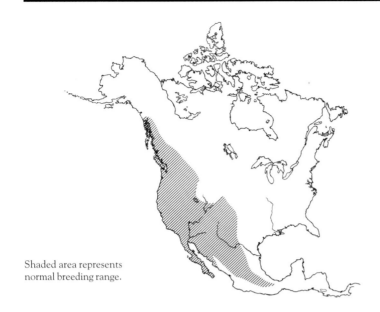

Shaded area represents normal breeding range.

**STATISTICS**

| | |
|---|---|
| STATUS: | common |
| LENGTH: | 19-27.5 cm. (7.5-11 in.) |
| WINGSPAN: | 46-61 cm. (18-24 in.) |
| MASS: | male 88-178 gm. (~3-6 oz.); female 92-220 gm. |
| LIFESPAN: | up to 13 yrs. |
| CLUTCH: | 2-8 |
| EGGS: | white; oval to round; ~36 x 31 mm. (1.4 x 1.2 in.) |
| INCUBATION: | 26 days |
| FLEDGING: | 28 days |

**M**ost Western Screech Owls are indistinguishable from their eastern counterpart except in voice. Western Screech Owls are slightly larger on average and only rarely exhibit a red phase. They occupy the same ecological niche as the Eastern Screech Owl and are only controversially designated a separate species.

## OTHER ENGLISH NAMES
See Eastern Screech Owl

## DIMORPHISM
A phase of less red occurs, albeit rarely, but is less intense than that of the eastern species occurs.

## DISTRIBUTION
The Western Screech Owl's range extends as far north as extreme southern Alaska and is confined to west of the Rocky Mountains. The range extends south through British Columbia to Baja, California and western Mexico.

## HABITAT
As with their eastern relatives, Western Screech Owls prefer open woodland and scrub brush over densely forested areas. Such habitats include the damp coastal conifer forests of the Pacific Northwest to cottonwood groves of the western interior to saguaro deserts and dry pine and juniper forests.

## SUBSPECIES
The darkest races of the Western Screech Owl are found in the wet Pacific northwestern coastal forests. *Otus kennicottii kennicottii*, the darkest form, lives in British Columbia on the Queen Charlotte Islands and the coastal mainland. Paler forms are found in desert areas. *O. k. cinerascens* is the palest race, in Baja, California and the dry western plains. The largest race (*O. k. macfarlanei*) inhabits the interior of British Columbia and Oregon, and the smallest (*O. k. xanthusi*) inhabits Baja California.

## VOICE
The most commonly heard song or territorial call is often referred to as the "bouncing ball" call and may be used by both sexes simultaneously. This call consists of a string of soft hoots of the same pitch uttered increasingly close together until terminating with a rolling trill, hence the "bouncing ball" analogy. Other calls include whistled barks and meows similar to those of the Eastern Screech Owl.

## BREEDING HABITS
Same as the Eastern Screech Owl

## MIGRATION
Similar to the Eastern Screech Owl

## PREY
Similar to that of the Eastern Screech Owl

JW '97
Full-sized Western Screech Owl

# Western Screech Owl

**Note:** This plate also represents the
grey phase of the Eastern Screech Owl.

**Scale: 85%**

# Whiskered Owl

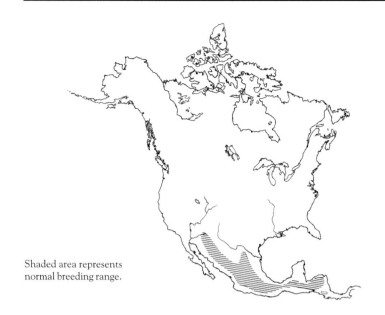

Shaded area represents normal breeding range.

**STATISTICS**

| | |
|---|---|
| STATUS: | uncommon |
| LENGTH: | 16-20 cm. (6.5-8 in.) |
| WINGSPAN: | 30-50 cm. (16-20 in.) |
| MASS: | male avg. 85 gm.; |
| | female avg. 92 gm. (~3 oz.) |
| CLUTCH: | 3-4 |
| EGGS: | white; oval to round; |
| | ~33 x 28 mm. (1.3x1.1 in.) |
| INCUBATION: | unknown |
| FLEDGING: | unknown |

The Whiskered Owl is similar in appearance to, though smaller than, its cohabitating relative, the Western Screech Owl. It is generally more boldly marked with greater contrast and larger streaking over much of its plumage. Its real telltale features gave rise to its name, where six elongated bristles, instead of three in the Common Screech Owls, extend well beyond the bill. More elongate bristles radiate about the facial discs. A reddish morph of the Whiskered Owl exists but is found only south of the United States/Mexico border.

**OTHER ENGLISH NAMES**
Spotted screech owl

**DIMORPHISM**
The female is slightly larger on average.

**DISTRIBUTION**
The Whiskered Owl's range extends north barely into southern Arizona and New Mexico, and south through mountainous regions of Mexico, and Central America to Honduras.

**HABITAT**
Often found near running water, the Whiskered Owl lives on heavily forested mountain slopes, in canyons, coffee plantations, and groves of oak and sycamore.

**SUBSPECIES**
Between 3 and 7 subspecies of the Whiskered Owl are currently recognized. The only race extending north into the United States is *Otus trichopsis asperus*. This race is the greyest of all forms (others having more reddish-brown coloration), has no red morph, and has well-feathered rather than bristled toes.

**VOICE**
Territorial calls of the Whiskered Owl consist of a series of 3 to 4 short, consecutive monotone notes... boot-boot-boot. The female's call is higher-pitched than the male's. The mating call can be described as Morse code-like, exchanged during courtship by male and female in single, double and inconsistently accented notes. Other calls consist of whistles, meows and shrieks.

**BREEDING HABITS**
Little is known of the breeding habits of the Whiskered Owl. They are known, however, to be very territorial. Nests have been found in the cavities and vacant woodpecker holes of sycamores, oaks and juniper stumps. Clutch size is usually 3 to 4 eggs.

**MIGRATION**
Resident

**PREY**
The Whiskered Owl feeds mostly on arthropods but occasionally takes small mammals, birds, reptiles and amphibians. Of the invertebrates, orthopterans, coleopterans and lepidopterans represent the majority, while spiders, scorpions and centipedes are regularly caught.

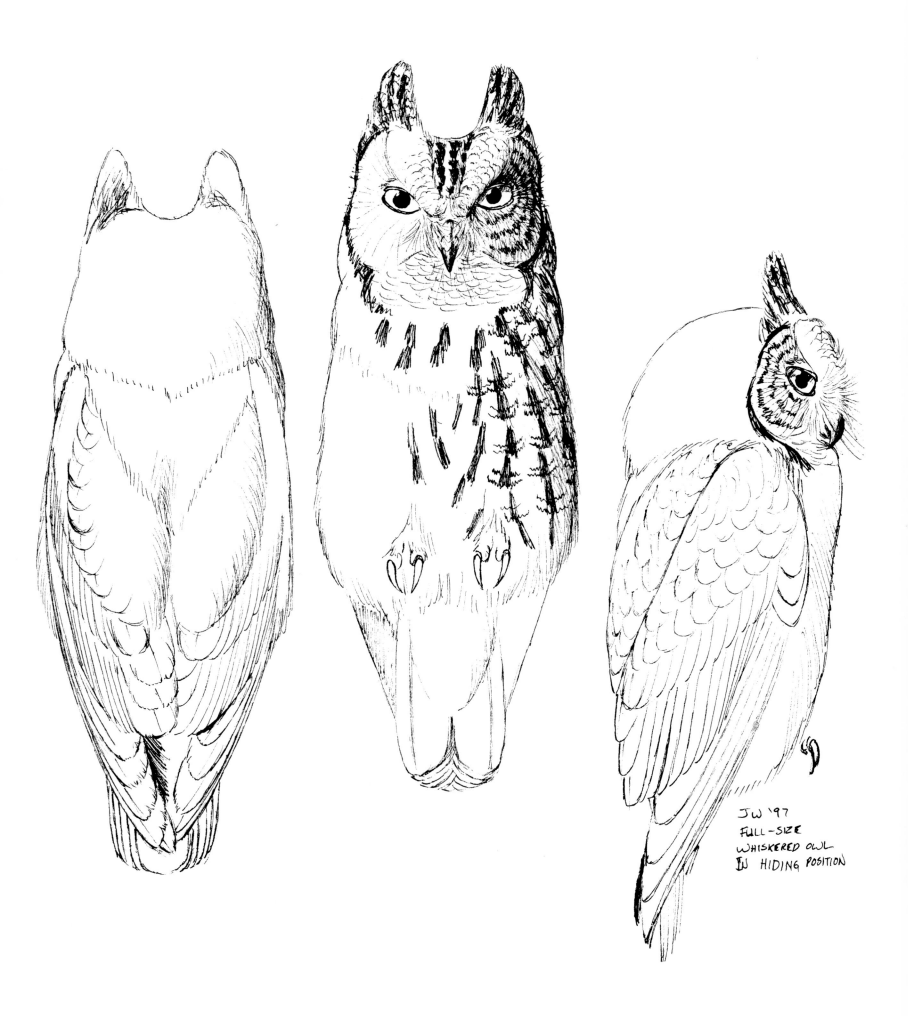

JW '97
FULL-SIZE
WHISKERED OWL
IN HIDING POSITION

# Whiskered Owl

**Scale: 100%**

# Great Horned Owl

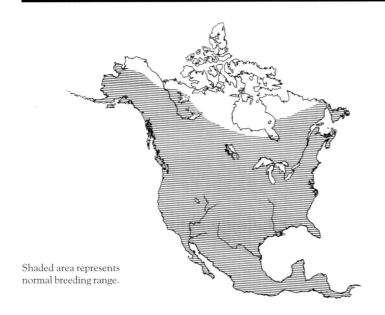

Shaded area represents
normal breeding range.

STATISTICS
STATUS:        common
LENGTH:        46-63 cm. (18-25 in.)
WINGSPAN:      125-150 cm. (50-60 in.)
MASS:          .7 - 2.5 kg.(1.5-5.5 lb.);
               male avg. ~1.3 kg.(3 lb.);
               female avg. ~1.75 kg. ( 4 lb.)
LIFESPAN:      up to 29 years (in captivity)
CLUTCH:        generally 2-3, up to 6
EGGS:          white; oval; ~56 x 47 mm.
               ( 2.2x2 in.)
INCUBATION:    26-34 days
FLEDGING:      63 to 70 days

The Great Horned Owl is the most powerful of all North American owl species, although the Great Gray Owl is larger in dimension, and the Snowy Owl may have greater mass. It has large ear tufts, usually displayed prominently, and well-defined facial discs (sienna with bold dark border). Colouration is cryptic and extremely variable geographically, paralleling backgrounds these owls would be expected to be seen against. Eyes are straw to orange-yellow in color. A notable field mark is a broad, white throat patch. Legs and claws are very sturdy.

The Great Horned Owl is a largely nocturnal and highly territorial predator. Most of the day is spent roosting and avoiding the mobbing of corvid flocks. It typically adopts a cryptic upright posture with ear tufts held erect. It is an opportunistic feeder at night, with the most varied diet of all owls or any other bird of prey in North America. Great Horned Owls are generally not subject to predation, although they are known to feed on many other cohabitating species of owl. The Great Horned Owl has a ferocious disposition and will defend its nest fearlessly.

### OTHER ENGLISH NAMES
Virginia horned owl; horned owl; hoot owl; big hoot owl; cat owl; chicken owl; eagle owl; king owl; big duke owl

### DIMORPHISM
Females are approximately 30% larger than males.

### DISTRIBUTION
The Great Horned Owl is found throughout most of the Americas, south of the subarctic treeline.

### HABITAT
Exceedingly variable, it includes virtually all habitats existing within the American continents from sea level to 3300 m or 11, 000 feet (up to 4100 m in South America). They are found virtually anywhere that there are trees and rocky terrain, roosting in old nest sites, among dense foliage, within tree cavities and equivalently on rocky ledges and sheltered high points.

### SUBSPECIES
The Great Horned Owl's plumage varies greatly over its North American range, where geographic isolation has led to subspeciation. The lightest-colored races occur in the northern extreme of the Canadian Shield (*Bubo virginianus subarcticus*), almost mistakable for a Snowy

Owl, and in Arizona to northwestern Mexico (*B. v. pallascens*). The darkest and most heavily marked races occur in the western temperate rainforests (*B. v. saturatus*) and in north-eastern Canada (northern Quebec, Newfoundland and Labrador) (*B. v. heterocnemus*). As many as nineteen subspecies have been described throughout their New World range.

### VOICE
The male's territorial call is a series of deep, resonant hoots, typically starting with a single loud hoot, followed immediately by a small number of staccato hoots, with the sequence terminating in two further full hoots... HOO-hoo-hoo-hoo-HOO-HOO. Female call/response is similar but higher pitched. Variations of this occur as warning calls, intermixed with more aggressive hissing, growling, groaning, squealing, bill-clapping, and rarely a blood-curdling scream. Sexual calls include cries, meows, groaning and laughter.

### BREEDING HABITS
More often than not, Great Horned Owls occupy the abandoned treetop nests of other birds of prey, particularly that of the Red-tailed Hawk. They also commonly nest in rocky nooks and ledges. Very occasionally, they will nest on the ground in tall grass or at the foot of a tree

trunk. It usually takes two years for a Great Horned Owl to reach sexual maturity.

Courtship usually begins very early in the winter and involves mutual preening, wild calls, bill-rubbing, and strange dances in which the white throat is expanded, wings droop, the tail is cocked and the birds strut about. Eggs are also laid early (January-February in the northern United States), often with snow still on the ground. A female Great Horned Owl will lay anywhere from one to six eggs per nesting, but most commonly 2 to 3. Incubation is performed by both parents, with the female doing most of the incubating and the male spending most of his time hunting and providing food. Incubation lasts 26 to 34 days. The young remain in the nest for 5 to 6 weeks and are capable of flight after 63 to 70 days.

## MIGRATION

These owls are largely sedentary with year-long established territories which may last several consecutive years. Outside breeding season some may wander great distances. Individuals in the far north may follow prey abundance southward during particularly harsh winters.

## PREY

The Great Horned Owl hunts from a perch, primarily from a conspicuous vantage point (tree tops, telephone poles, rock ledges). It is an opportunistic and versatile feeder. The proportions of prey type vary considerably from locale to locale and are affected by cyclic fluctuations of prey populations.

Mammals account for the vast majority of the Great Horned Owl's diet, followed by birds of almost any type (a distant second), including owls and hawks, other vertebrates and arthropods. Of the mammals, rabbits, hares, rats and small microtine rodents (including small voles and mice) are favoured. Less frequent but known prey include skunks, porcupines, opossums, weasels, foxes, domestic cats and bats. Domestic fowl are also frequent targets. Among the other vertebrates which make up the great horned's diet, are snakes (including venomous), lizards and frogs and other amphibians and fish. Arthropod prey taken is also extremely varied, including insects such as crickets, beetles, grasshoppers, arachnids and various crustaceans.

JW '97
1/3 sized
GREAT HORNED OWL

# Great Horned Owl

# Northern Hawk Owl

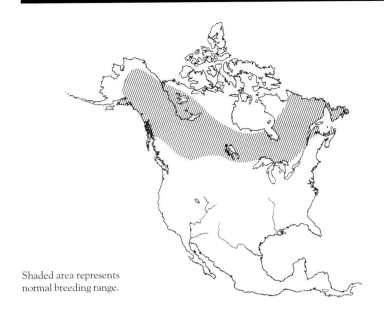

Shaded area represents
normal breeding range.

STATISTICS
STATUS:        locally common
LENGTH:        36-44cm. (14.5-17.5 in.);
               tail ~17 cm. (7 in.)
WINGSPAN:      80-90 cm. (31-35 in.)
MASS: male     ~350 gm. (12 oz.);
               female ~400 gm. (14 oz.)
CLUTCH:        3-13
EGGS:          glossy white
INCUBATION:    28 days
FLEDGING:      unknown

As its name implies, the Northern Hawk Owl is an owl which possesses many of the apparent characteristics of a hawk. Most notably it has a very long tail and relatively pointed wings, so particularly in flight, this species appears more similar to other diurnal birds of prey than to other members of its taxonomic family. The body plumage of the Northern Hawk Owl is stiffer than the downy frontal feathers of other boreal species of owls. The facial discs are uniformly pale and relatively small, but heavily bordered by dark "sideburns" and fainter "beard". These dark markings also continue around the side and back of the head. The relatively small eyes are yellow with an angered expression. The bill is a light yellowish tone. It is heavily barred over its front, and its body and wings have dark upper sides. The crown and scapulars are most heavily marked in white.

## OTHER ENGLISH NAMES
American hawk owl; Canadian owl; Hudsonian owl

## DIMORPHISM
Male and females are indistinguishable except for their average differences in weight.

## DISTRIBUTION
Holarctic. The breeding range is almost totally confined to the taiga, which in North America extends north to the treeline from Alaska to Labrador and just south of this biome to the mixed woodlands of southern Canada including British Columbia, the prairie provinces, Ontario, southern Quebec and New Brunswick, and the north central states of Minnesota, Wisconsin and Michigan.

## HABITAT
The Northern Hawk Owl is found throughout the taigan biome of North America, where it prefers the open coniferous woods, burnt lands and bogs or muskeg in particular. It is also comfortable in the mixed forests just south of the boreal forest region.

## SUBSPECIES
Only one subspecies is recognized in North America, *Surnia ulula caparoch*, It is darker than its old world relatives.

## VOICE
Known for its name-giving rolling trill, the vociferous Northern Hawk Owl also has a variety of other calls in its repertoire. Most commonly heard is the male's territorial and courtship call... U-lulululululululu. Alarm calls can vary from raspy screeches to throaty squawks. It also utters hisses, yips and rattles.

## BREEDING HABITS
Nest sites are chosen either in broken spruce hollows or other tree cavities including woodpecker holes. Occasionally, they will nest in an old crow or hawk nest. Clutch size is heavily dependent on the abundance of food during breeding time and as a result is highly variable. In harsh times, breeding may not even occur, but when it does, the number of eggs laid may be as few as 3. When prey are abundant as many as 13 may be laid. Incubation responsibilities are generally relegated to the female although the male may have some. Most of the time, though, the male hunts for the nestlings and their mother.

## MIGRATION
Hawk owls generally migrate south during winters to the northern tier of the United States.

### PREY

Hawk owls require high perches in open woodland to survey the area for rodents. They are very swift fliers and will move regularly from perch to perch, usually a dead spruce tree.

The Northern Hawk Owl's prey of choice are small rodents, consisting of voles, bog lemmings and shrews. Mice, chipmunks, ground squirrels, flying squirrels, rats, large insects and frogs are taken when the former are in short supply. When the abundance of food is further reduced, hawk owls will take numerous species of birds including ptarmigan and grouse, ducks and various boreal species of songbirds.

JW '97
½ SIZE
NORTHERN HAWK OWL

# Northern Hawk Owl

**Scale: 54%**

# Northern Pygmy Owl

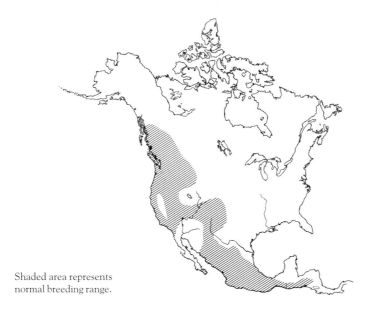

Shaded area represents
normal breeding range.

| STATISTICS | |
|---|---|
| STATUS: | locally common |
| LENGTH: | 18-19 cm. (7-7.5 in.) |
| WINGSPAN: | 37-41 cm. (14.5-16 in.) |
| MASS: | male avg. 62 gm. (2 oz.).; |
| | female avg. 73 gm. (2.5 oz) |
| CLUTCH: | 2-7 |
| EGGS: | white; ~26.5 x 23 mm. |
| | (1 x 1.1 in.) |
| INCUBATION: | 28 days |
| FLEDGING: | 28 days |

A very small and very tame, earless owl of western North America, the Northern Pygmy Owl is a diurnal predator. The basic body color ranges from a reddish-brown burnt umber to a greyer-brown raw umber. Most of the dark plumes are marked with small white spots, generally in the centre of each feather. The belly is white with bold striping down the centre of the elongated feathers, while the chest continues the coloration of the upper parts. The Northern Pygmy Owl has small facial discs with a light brow continuing over the yellowish bill. The eyes are yellow. Of particular interest is a second pair of "eyes" on the nape. These false eyes are oversized and dark with a white border. Wings are relatively pointed and flight is rapid and hawklike. The tail is comparatively long and boldly barred with white.

The Northern Pygmy Owl feeds on a vast diversity of prey during the day, many of which exceed the owl's tiny size. At night it roosts under protection of dense cover or within a tree cavity, avoiding the hungry eyes of larger owls. It is a fierce and fearless hunter when supporting a family, killing a wide variety of perching birds and others as large as grouse. Not too surprisingly, the Northern Pygmy Owl is subject to severe harassment and mobbing by other birds.

## OTHER ENGLISH NAMES
Gnome owl

## DIMORPHISM
Sexes are virtually indistinguishable in the field. Females are, on average, larger and heavier.

## DISTRIBUTION
The Northern Pygmy Owl is found year-round within and west of the central mountains in British Columbia, extending north as far as the extreme southern Alaskan coast, south through the mountains of California, the Baja peninsula to the highlands of Mexico and Guatemala.

## HABITAT
Northern Pygmy Owls favor the open coniferous forests of the interior mountains to the moist coastal forests in the Pacific northwest. They also inhabit open oak and pine forests and other clearings such as alpine meadows. They are typically found between 400 and 3000 m above sea level.

## SUBSPECIES
Seven subspecies of Northern Pygmy Owls are widely recognized. Of these the largest tend to be farthest north, with *Glaucidium gnoma pinicola* of the Rocky Mountains being the largest and *G. g. gnoma* of Mexico being the smallest. The other major trend is with darkness of plumage; inland birds tend to be lighter in coloration than their coastal relatives. The darkest form (*G. g. swarthi*) is found on Vancouver Island and the lightest (*G. g. hoskinsii*) in Baja California.

## VOICE
The most commonly uttered call consists of several evenly spaced dovelike coos, either singly or in pairs... *coo-coo-coo* or *coo-coo, coo-coo, coo-coo...* Other calls include whinnying, whistling and trills.

## BREEDING HABITS
The vast majority of nest sites are chosen in vacant woodpecker holes, although natural tree cavities are also used. Breeding usually occurs between April and June and in-

cubation of the 2 to 7 eggs typically lasts 28 days. Incubation is performed by the female. Young fledge at approximately 28 days.

## MIGRATION

Northern Pygmy Owls are largely resident but generally descend from high altitudes during harsh winter conditions.

## PREY

Large insects and vertebrates other than mammals or birds constitute most of the Northern Pygmy Owl's prey. Among the insects, grasshoppers, crickets, katydids, bee-

tles, cicadas, dragonflies as well as butterflies and moths form its diet. The owls also take numerous species of frogs, lizards and small snakes. Mammals regularly taken include a variety of voles, mice, chipmunks and pocket gophers. Of the wide variety of birds that the Northern Pygmy Owl hunts and kills, most are small perching birds. Other more ambitious prey includes quail and grouse.

JW '97
FULL-SIZED
NORTHERN PYGMY OWL

# Northern Pygmy Owl

Scale: 100%

# Ferruginous Pygmy Owl

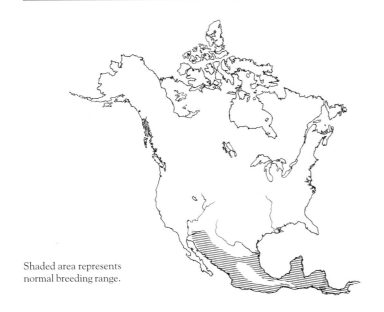

Shaded area represents
normal breeding range.

**STATISTICS**

| | |
|---|---|
| STATUS: | locally common to scarce |
| LENGTH: | 16-18 cm. (6.5-7 in.) |
| WINGSPAN: | 37-41 cm. (14.5-16 in.) |
| MASS: | male avg. 62 gm. (2 oz.); female avg. 75 gm. (3 oz.) |
| CLUTCH: | 3-4 |
| EGGS: | white; ~ 29 x 24 mm. (1.1 x .9 in) |
| INCUBATION: | 28 days |
| FLEDGING: | 27-30 days |

Indistinguishable in size and shape and very similar in coloration to its close relative the Northern Pygmy Owl, the Ferruginous Pygmy Owl is also a daytime hunter. Its feathers are less harshly marked than its northern relative. Instead of sharply contrasting spots on the crown, the light markings are more elongate and blended. The best fieldmark distinguishing the two species is that the tail of the Ferruginous Pygmy Owl has eight to ten white bars on an always reddish-brown tail, whereas the Northern Pygmy Owl has at most eight, which it characteristically flicks up and lowers.

## OTHER ENGLISH NAMES
Ferruginous owl; gnome owl

## DIMORPHISM
Females are larger than males

## DISTRIBUTION
Ferruginous Pygmy Owl populations occupy subtropical and tropical America from the extreme southern United States, in Arizona and Texas, south, discontinuously through Central and South America.

## HABITAT
Ferruginous Pygmy Owls live in dry subtropical to tropical environments, occupying open woods, scrub brush, grasslands, saguaro deserts and other human-induced clearings. They can be found breeding anywhere from sea level to 3000 m elevation.

## SUBSPECIES
There are several recognized races of Ferruginous Pygmy Owl, distinguished largely by coloration and the presence or absence of different color morphs. In the northernmost extent of their range, the extreme southern United States, there are two representative subspecies.

*Glaucidium brasilianum cactorum*, of Arizona and *G. b. ridgwayi*, of Texas, occupy the northernmost extent of the range.

## VOICE
Same as the Northern Pygmy Owl.

## BREEDING HABITS
Ferruginous Pygmy Owls are versatile nesters, choosing sites in a wide range of sheltered spaces. Cavities in trees and saguaro cacti and vacant woodpecker holes are common nest sites. Clutch size is usually 3 to 4 and subject to the availability of food. Females incubate for approximately 28 days while the male hunts and provides food. Fledging occurs after 27-30 days.

## MIGRATION
Generally accepted to be resident year-round.

## PREY
Most of the Ferruginous Pygmy Owl's prey consists of large insects, particularly orthopterans, large moths, cicadas and beetles. Scorpions are also regularly killed and eaten. Small birds form a small portion of its diet as do lizards. Small mammals are only occasionally taken.

JW '97
FULL-SIZE
FERRUGINOUS PYGMY OWL

# Ferruginous Pygmy Owl

Scale: 100%

# Elf Owl

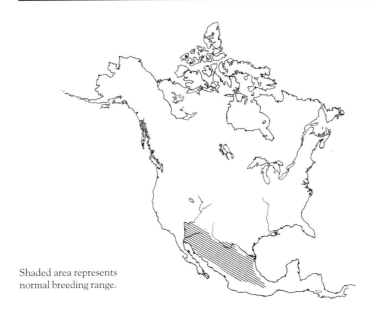

Shaded area represents
normal breeding range.

| STATISTICS | |
| --- | --- |
| STATUS: | locally threatened |
| LENGTH: | 130-140 mm. ( 5-6 in.) |
| WINGSPAN: | 34-42 cm. (13.5-16.5 in.) |
| MASS: | 35-55 gm. (1.2-2 oz) |
| LIFESPAN: | 7 years (in captivity) |
| TERRITORY: | >10 m. (30 ft.)dia. (food dependent) |
| CLUTCH: | 1-5 |
| EGGS: | white; ~23 x 20 mm. (.9 x .8 in.) |
| INCUBATION: | 24 days (May - June) |
| FLEDGING: | 28-33 days |

The Elf Owl is the smallest species of owl in the world - with the diminutive mass of only 40 g or 1.5 oz. It is energetic, insectivorous, hornless and nocturnal. Typically inhabiting hot environments, the Elf Owl remains hidden in dense vegetation or in a woodpecker hole during the day. Characteristically, it does not possess the feather structure necessary to enable silent flight. It is also the only North American owl to have only 10 rectrices instead of 12. It has a relatively weak bill and short tail. The Elf Owl is a general mottled grey with varying amounts of sienna. Except for white brows, the face is subtly marked. Its eyes are yellow and toes are sparsely feathered.

## OTHER ENGLISH NAMES
Whitney's owl

## DIMORPHISM
Males are, on average, smaller than females.

## DISTRIBUTION
Elf Owls are found in hot and dry desert areas of southern California, northern Colorado, southern Nevada, Arizona, New Mexico and southern Texas, south to Baja California and central Mexico.

## HABITAT
Elf Owls are desert dwellers. Saguaro cacti provide the little birds with their favoured nest sites. Groves of cottonwood and sycamores, dense thickets on dry mountain slopes and pine and oak woodlands, typically near running water, are also popular environments. They have been found nesting up to 2000 m (6500 ft.) above sea level.

## SUBSPECIES
Four subspecies of Elf Owl are recognized. Each is distinguished by subtle variations in coloration (darkness and color intensity).

## VOICE
The Elf Owl produces a variety of calls. It is also very capable, for its size, of projecting its voice. The territorial song consists of a series of rapid, high-pitched notes *tchew-tchew-tchew*.

## BREEDING Habits
Elf Owls nest predominantly in the vacant woodpecker holes of saguaro cacti, although they regularly choose sites in natural or woodpecker-excavated cavities in various local trees such as cottonwoods, oak and pine. Up to five eggs are laid, in April to May, and are incubated by both male and female for approximately 24 days. Young fledge after 28 to 33 days.

## MIGRATION
Elf Owls occupying the northern portion of their range fly southward, usually in October, for winter.

## PREY
The Elf Owl feeds only on insects and other arthropods. In particular, orthopterans (including locust, grasshopper, cricket etc.) make up a large portion of its diet, but other insects such as large moths, beetles, centipedes, spiders and scorpions are also important prey.

JW'97    FULL-SIZED ELF OWL

# Elf Owl

Scale: 100%

# Burrowing Owl

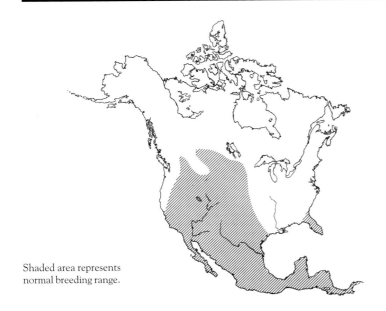

Shaded area represents
normal breeding range.

| STATISTICS | |
|---|---|
| STATUS: | threatened |
| LENGTH: | 23-28 cm. ( 9-11 in.) |
| WINGSPAN: | 50-60 cm. (20-24 in.) |
| MASS: | male avg. 160 gm.; |
| | female avg. 150 gm. ( ~5 oz) |
| LIFESPAN: | 11 years (in captivity) |
| TERRITORY: | >4 ha or 10 acres |
| CLUTCH size: | 6-11 |
| EGGS: | white |
| INCUBATION: | 28 days |

A medium-sized diurnal owl, the Burrowing Owl is a curious bird both in appearance and in habit. On the prairies and grasslands, they live in small colonies in underground burrows. They spend much of their time moving about on two legs, even running down prey. In the North American short-grass prairies they coexist among prairie dog colonies where their population densities can be as high as one breeding pair per 10 acres (4 ha). When not associated with prairie dog colonies, the population densities drop significantly. Hunting occurs from the highest available observation point as is available, usually a fencepost or a prairie dog hill. When disturbed in their burrow, young Burrowing Owls often mimic the sounds of an irate rattlesnake. Burrowing Owls are subject to predation by coyotes, bobcats, badgers, weasels, skunks and rattlesnakes.

The Burrowing Owl is brown to sand colored and heavily marked in white spots and bars over most of its plumage. It has a scowling facial expression, though not quite as fierce-looking as the pygmy owls. They have long, sparsely feathered tarsi and toes and a relatively small head with reduced facial discs. Their eyes are yellow to straw and their bill is usually a light straw color.

## OTHER ENGLISH NAMES
Billy owl; prairie dog owl; prairie owl; ground owl

## DIMORPHISM
Indistinguishable except male is slightly larger on average.

## DISTRIBUTION
Found throughout the Americas in regions of expansive grasslands and other open, dry areas. It breeds as far north as southwestern Canada in southern British Columbia, Alberta, Saskatchewan and Manitoba. It is found only accidently in southeastern Canada. In the United States it breeds primarily in the midwest and western states but maintains populations as far east as Florida and the Bahamas. It breeds and lives in grasslands throughout the Americas all the way to Tierra del Fuego.

## HABITAT
Burrowing Owls live in expansive open areas of grasslands, sagebrush and near desert conditions. In their central and South American range, they occupy savannas and alpine grasslands up to 4000 m altitude. They have broadened their geographical range by taking advantage of artificial clearings such as airports, farmland and golf courses.

## SUBSPECIES
Up to twenty subspecies of Burrowing Owls are recognized over their Pan-American range, distinguished primarily by coloration, size and geographic isolation. North American birds represent two subspecies. A particularly dark form (*Athene cunicularia floridana*) is limited to a small region in Florida, while *A. c. hypugaea* occupies the rest of the species' North American range.

## VOICE
The Burrowing Owl's primary call is a clear but soft Cooo-Coooo! A rattling call is often uttered by young when disturbed, from within the burrow, presumably to mimic a rattlesnake. Other sounds include chattering, cackling and shrieks.

## BREEDING HABITS
The Burrowing Owl nests in small colonies underground, usually in abandoned prairie dog or other burrows, although it is capable of excavating its own. The nest is lined with plant matter as a protective cushion for the

clutch of 6 to 11 eggs. Incubation lasts approximately 28 days.

## MIGRATION

Individuals living and breeding in the northernmost regions migrate south in winter. As well, Burrowing Owls descend from high altitudes during winter months .

## PREY

Invertebrates, insects in particular, form the vast majority of the Burrowing Owl's diet. Small mammals are a regular, if less frequent, food. Reptiles and amphibians, including snakes, lizards and toads are also taken. Small birds are only rarely part of the Burrowing Owl's meal plan. Proportions of the diet constituents vary according to region, and due to their wide distribution, the list of species taken for food is quite long. Of the insects, the most common prey include ground beetles, locusts, mole crickets and dung beetles. Other invertebrate prey include centipedes, millipedes and various arachnids, including scorpions. Prairie dogs, ground squirrels, pocket gophers, voles, several species of mice, cottontail rabbits and jackrabbits are the most commonly taken mammals. The Burrowing Owl will also occasionally take any local bird which it can subdue.

JW '97
85% LIFESIZE
BURROWING OWL

# Burrowing Owl

Scale: 85%

# Spotted Owl

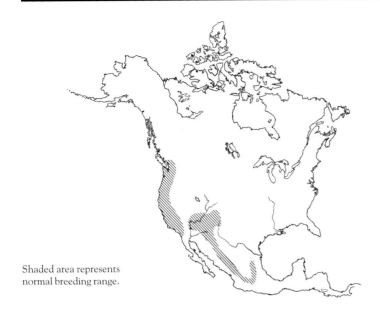

Shaded area represents
normal breeding range.

| STATISTICS | |
|---|---|
| STATUS: | threatened to locally endangered |
| LENGTH: | 42-48 cm. ( 16.5-19 in.) |
| WINGSPAN: | 100-125 cm. (40-50 in.) |
| MASS: | male avg. 580 gm.(1.3 lb); |
| | female avg. 640 gm. (1.4 lb) |
| CLUTCH: | 2-4 |
| EGGS: | white; elliptical to oval; |
| | ~50 x 41 mm. (1.9x1.6 in) |
| INCUBATION: | Unknown |
| FLEDGING: | Unknown |

Very similar in size and shape as well as being a close relative to the Barred Owl, the Spotted Owl is more densely and darkly feathered with spots rather than stripes on the underside. Spotted Owls are very rare and typically roost very high in light-deprived areas beneath the canopy. When located, they are quite tame and will allow a close approach. They have a very restricted range, limited to old-growth forests of western North America. It is due to this fact that so much controversy has surrounded this owl. Human residents of the Pacific northwest are quite aware of the impact this owl is having on the lives of loggers and logging companies.

Like the Barred Owl, the Spotted Owl has friendly dark brown eyes. Strangely, though, at close range the eyes appear a beautiful deep blue-violet - almost black. The bill is a straw color. Markings on the cape, scapular, wing coverts and rump are clear and contrasting but seem to be freeform in nature. The outermost row of scapulars are strongly marked in white. Flight feathers and tail feathers are clearly barred. Small spots on the forehead and crown blend to larger lateral bars on the nape and side of the head. Barred spots on the throat blend to doubly spotted feathers on the belly.

## DIMORPHISM
Females are on average only slightly larger than males.

## DISTRIBUTION
Spotted Owls are limited to a small discontinuous range in western North America. They are found from extreme southwestern British Columbia south to northwestern California, and, inland through the Sierra Nevada, Utah, central Colorado, the mountains of New Mexico, western Texas and central Mexico.

## HABITAT
Spotted Owls inhabit dense old-growth and mature forests from sea level to 2700 m altitude. They are typically found in the coastal forests of coniferous giants and in dark, damp canyons, usually near running water.

## SUBSPECIES
Up to four races of Spotted Owl are recognized, distinguished largely by geographic isolation.

## VOICE
Calls of the Spotted Owl are quite similar to the Barred Owl but slightly muted. The territorial call consists of a series of 3 to 4 soft but loud hoots with an accent on the last hoot " WHOO-WHOO-WHOO-WHOOO". Another common vocalization involves a hair-raising series of HOOs and HAAs evoking the image of a laughing demon crossed with a yelping coyote. Also performed commonly is an abruptly terminating harsh rising whistle.

## BREEDING HABITS
Most nesting sites are dark, cool areas in tree cavities, hollow stumps, recesses of cliff or cave walls or the abandoned nests of ravens, crows, hawks or Golden Eagles. Little is known about the actual breeding habits of this rare and reclusive bird.

## MIGRATION
Completely resident.

## PREY
Prey taken by Spotted Owls is essentially as varied as that taken by the Barred Owl and includes various species of birds including the Saw-whet Owl. Flying Squirrels, moles, shrews, mice, tree mice, woodrats, at least three species of bats, rabbits and pika make up most of its mammalian diet. Invertebrates represent a major portion of the Spot-

ted Owl's meal plan and will include a diverse selection of beetles, orthopterans, and large moths. Other vertebrates such as frogs and toads are an important part of its diet.

JW '97
½ SIZE   SPOTTED OWL

# Spotted Owl

Scale: 41%

# Barred Owl

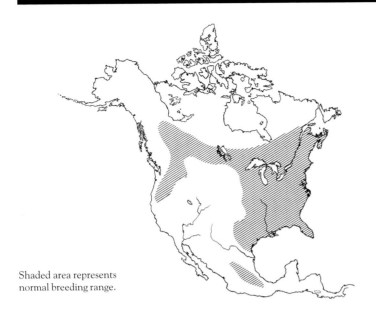

Shaded area represents
normal breeding range.

| STATISTICS | |
|---|---|
| STATUS: | locally common |
| LENGTH: | 43-61 cm. (17-24 in.) |
| WINGSPAN: | 100-125 cm. (40-50 in.) |
| MASS: | male avg. 630 gm. (1.4 lb); |
| | female avg. 800 gm. (1.8 lb) |
| LIFESPAN: | 23 years in captivity |
| CLUTCH: | 2-4 |
| EGGS: | white; elliptical to oval; |
| | ~50 x 41 mm. (2 x 1.6 in.) |
| INCUBATION: | 28 days |
| FLEDGING: | 42 days |

The Barred Owl is a geographically widespread, medium to large-sized owl of nocturnal habit. It has dark brown eyes, lending it a friendly stare. Though generally quite tame to human approach, it will often react violently to unwelcomed visits to its nesting area.

Named for its extensive dark and light barring over much of its body (crown, nape, throat, cape, scapulars, tail and flight feathers), the plumage is largely a contrasting two-tone umber and white. It is a fierce predator, and will kill and eat most smaller owls. The bill is sturdy and light-yellowish often with a tinge of green. The belly is boldly striped with loose and elongate plumes.

## OTHER ENGLISH NAMES
Hoot owl; wood owl; swamp owl; rain owl; laughing owl; crazy owl; black-eyed owl

## DIMORPHISM
Females are larger on average than males but otherwise indistinguishable.

## DISTRIBUTION
The Barred Owl is found from northeastern British Columbia to northern California, north of the American western interior and midwest, across southern Canada, and south through the eastern United States to Mexico.

## HABITAT
They inhabit dense, mature, mixed and coniferous forests, swamps, near creeks, lakes and river valleys.

## SUBSPECIES
Four subspecies of Barred Owl are currently recognized. *Strix varia varia* of the north is generally the largest form. A smaller race, *S. v. georgia*, inhabits the humid southeastern states and a pale form, *S. v. helveola*, lives in the dry regions of Texas and Mexico.

## VOICE
The Barred Owl is the most vociferous of North American species. Its territorial call is a distinctive two-part series of HOOs and HAAs, often denoted "Who cooks for you? Who cooks for you all?" or more closely *how-HOO-ha-HOO!... how-HOO-ha-HOOAaahhh!*", sometimes ending in demonic laughter. In addition to this well-known song is a repertoire of hisses, shrieks, barks, yelps, cackles, moans and whistles.

## BREEDING HABITS
The most commonly chosen nest sites of Barred Owls are hollows of old trees and abandoned nests of hawks and crows. Pairs tend to return year after year to the same site. Two to 3 eggs are usually laid per clutch and incubated almost exclusively by the female for 28 days. Nestlings fledge after approximately 42 days.

## MIGRATION
Barred Owls are almost always year-round residents except during exceptionally harsh winter conditions, when they will move en masse to more favourable areas.

## PREY
The Barred Owl's diet is an extremely varied one composed mainly of mammals but including a significant proportion of birds, other vertebrates and arthropods. Of the mammals, mice, voles, woodrats, squirrels, shrews, chipmunks, opossums, rabbits, hares and bats are commonly taken. Avian prey include smaller owls, woodpeckers, crows, jays, kingfishers, grouse, doves, thrushes, sparrows, warblers, finches and swallows. Other prey include lizards, snakes, frogs, salamanders, slugs, beetles,

orthopterans, crustaceans and arachnids.  The Barred Owl
has also been known to have mastered fishing.

JW '97
HALF-SIZED
BARRED OWL

# Barred Owl

Scale: 41%

# Great Gray Owl

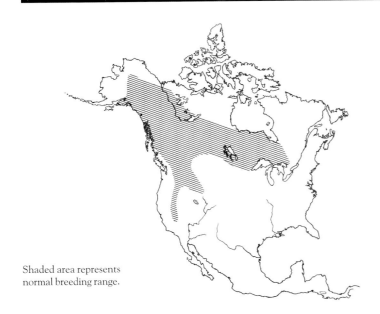

Shaded area represents
normal breeding range.

**STATISTICS**

| | |
|---|---|
| STATUS: | uncommon to rare |
| LENGTH: | 61-84 cm. (24-33 in.) |
| WINGSPAN: | 135-150 cm. (54-60 in.) |
| MASS: | male avg. 1 kg. (2 lb.); female avg. 1.3 kg. (3 lb.) |
| TERRITORY: | highly variable >.5 km² |
| CLUTCH: | 2-5 |
| EGGS: | white; oval; ~53 x 42 mm. (2.1 x 1.7 in.) |
| INCUBATION: | ~30 days |
| FLEDGING: | 21-28 days |

The Great Gray Owl is the largest of the North American owls and lacks ear tufts. With a mass of approximately a kilogram it is, on average, only two-thirds the weight of the dimensionally smaller Great Horned Owl. Although it is a very large bird, prey taken by the Great Gray Owl is quite small. They are active at dusk and dawn, roosting typically close to a large tree trunk during the brightest daylight hours and the darkest period of night. Although usually very tame, the Great Gray Owl may react with ferocity if encountered close to the nest site. It has been known to inflict serious wounds on human intruders.

The tail is proportionally very long and the wings are wide and squarish when spread. It has relatively small eyes and huge facial discs, giving a very flattened impression. The eyes are yellow to straw and the bill is straw-colored. The Great Gray Owl's plumage is cryptic and bland, with varying proportions of off-white and raw umber. The facial discs are emphasized by concentric dark/light patterns radiating away from the eyes, and are bordered by a small, dark ring of stiffer feathers. A white ridge of elongated feathers flows forward in front of the eyes and over much of the bill, blending to softer, white patches in the throat area, surrounding a darker patch leading down from the bill. The underparts are mottled but definitely streaked. The upper parts, including the wing coverts, are a combination of mottled barring, streaking and vermiculation. The tarsi and toes are heavily feathered, and mottled in coloration, and armed with very long claws.

## OTHER ENGLISH NAMES
Grey owl; spectral owl; spruce owl

## DIMORPHISM
Females have a significantly greater mass, on average, than males.

## DISTRIBUTION
The Great Gray Owl is an Holarctic species, found in boreal Eurasia as well as North America.

## HABITAT
Great Gray Owls are almost exclusively limited to the boreal forest biome, in muskeg, sphagnum bogs among spruce, tamarack and fir trees, and deciduous forests of aspen and poplar. In the southern mountainous areas of their range, they inhabit high altitudes in subalpine forests and meadows, up to 3200 m. (40,000 ft.)

## SUBSPECIES
Two subspecies of Great Gray Owl are recognized, one in North America and the other in the Old World.

## VOICE
The Great Gray Owl's territorial song consists of a string of soft but deep and loud hoots "WHOO-WHOO-WHOO-WHOO-WHOO-WHOO-WHOO" uttered by the male and answered by the female with a similar, solitary "WHOO". Courtship calls include screeching, cooing and whistling. Other calls include barks, rasping screeches and squawks.

## BREEDING HABITS
Nest sites of the Great Gray Owl are commonly chosen near clearings in among dense coniferous forest. Often, the abandoned nests of crows, ravens and birds of prey, old rotting stumps and occasionally ground sites are selected.

Courting entails food gifts from the male to the female, mutual preening, nuzzling and general grooming. The male will provide food for the female throughout the entire breeding period. Nesting may occur over a wide time window, but often begins while snow is still on the ground. The size of clutch is usually 3 eggs; however, as with many other species of owl, this is largely dependent on the availability of food. During tight times, breeding may be forgone altogether. The female is the sole undertaker of incubation, during which time she will only very rarely leave the nest. The male continues to feed her through the approximately 30-day incubation period. Nestlings typically fledge after 21 to 28 days.

## MIGRATION

The Great Gray Owl is sedentary except when food is unusually scarce. During these times they may move southward in great numbers. Irruptions seem to occur every 3 to 5 years.

## PREY

Small mammals compose virtually all of the Great Gray Owl's diet. It is particularly dependent upon *Microtus* voles, but feeds regularly on a wide variety of mice, shrews, moles, pocket gophers and weasels. Of lesser dietary significance are rats, squirrels, frogs, beetles and various birds, including grouse, ducks, crows and other smaller songbirds.

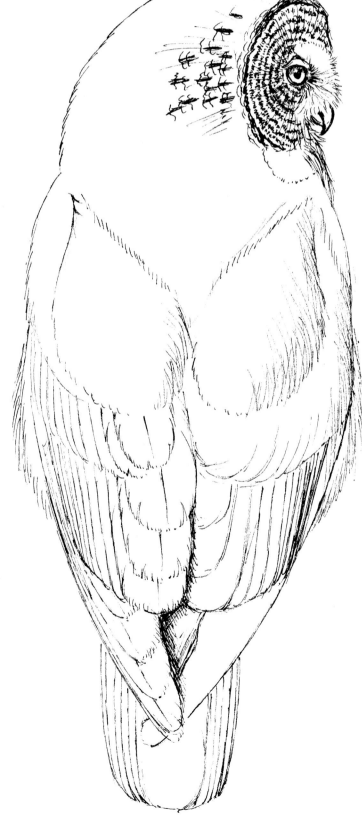

JW '97
⅓ SIZE
GREAT GRAY OWL

# Great Gray Owl

Scale: 33%

125

# Long-eared Owl

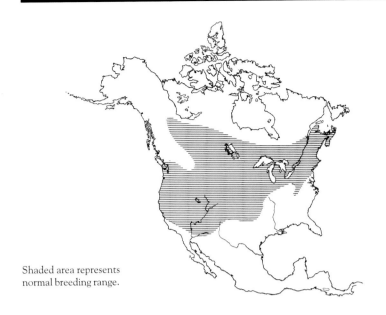

Shaded area represents normal breeding range.

**STATISTICS**

| | |
|---|---|
| STATUS: | locally common |
| LENGTH: | 350-400 mm. (13-16 in) |
| WINGSPAN: | 91-106 cm. (36-42 in) |
| MASS: | male average .25 kg. (9 oz); |
| | female average .280 kg. (10 oz) |
| LIFESPAN: | 27 years |
| TERRITORY: | none - gregarious and nomadic |
| CLUTCH: | 3-10 |
| EGGS: | glossy white; oval; |
| | ~40 x 32.5 mm. (1.6 x 1.3 in) |
| INCUBATION: | 26-28 days |
| FLEDGING: | 33-50 days (flight) |

The Long-eared Owl is a medium-sized Holarctic species with long ear tufts. Its overall coloration matches the description of the Great Horned Owl except that the long-eared is more boldly marked and has longitudinal stripes rather than transverse bars on the underside.

Long-eared Owls are very nocturnal. Daylight hours are spent roosting high in heavily foliated branches of conifers or alder, often gregariously, and very well camouflaged. If disturbed or threatened, the Long-eared Owl will inflate itself and fan its wings, hissing or screaming at the intruder. It will also aggressively defend an active nest site or perform a broken wing display to lead the threat away from the nest. Much of the long-eared's hunting occurs on the wing, high and low, cruising and hovering, typically over clearings.

## OTHER ENGLISH NAMES
American long-eared owl; Wilson's owl; cat owl; lesser horned owl

## DIMORPHISM
Females are slightly larger than males.

## DISTRIBUTION
Holarctic. In North America they breed almost as far north as the subarctic treeline in the southern Northwest Territories, south through inland British Columbia to Baja California, Arizona, west Texas and Nuevo Leon, Mexico, east through Oklahoma, Arkansas, Virginia, the Canadian prairie provinces and northern Ontario and all areas in between. They are also found in the Canadian maritimes and New England.

## HABITAT
Long-eared Owls inhabit coniferous and deciduous forest edges.

## SUBSPECIES
At least two subspecies of Long-eared Owl are recognized in North America. The most widespread is *Asio otus wilsonianus* and is differentiated from a southwestern Manitoban race by its darker coloration.

## VOICE
The Long-eared Owl has a wide range of vocalizations. The most common of these is the male territorial call, consisting of long single or double hoots.

## BREEDING HABITS
Long-eared Owls most commonly nest in the vacated nests of other predatory birds, corvids or herons and rarely on the ground. Breeding begins as early as February and incubation is solely the responsibility of the female. Males supply food to the incubating female and offspring. As many as ten eggs will be laid in a clutch; however, a typical clutch size is 3 to 5. The incubation period lasts 26 to 28 days. Young may leave the nest as soon as 20 days after hatching but usually make their first flight at about 34 days old.

## MIGRATION
The Long-eared Owl is actually not a resident of any particular spot, except during nesting. The rest of the year is spent leading a nomadic, rather than predictably migratory, lifestyle.

## PREY
The Long-eared Owl feeds primarily on small mammals such as voles, mice, rats, shrews, bog lemmings, chip-

munks, pocket gophers, moles, bats, small rabbits and squirrels. To a lesser extent, these owls feed on a wide variety of birds - anything easily caught. Insects, frogs and fish are also rarely taken.

JW '97
Half-sized
Long-eared Owl

# Long-eared Owl

Scale: 46%

# Short-eared Owl

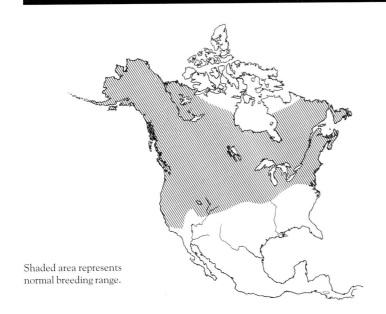

Shaded area represents
normal breeding range.

**STATISTICS**

| | |
|---|---|
| STATUS: | locally common |
| LENGTH: | 330-430 mm. (13-17 in.) |
| WINGSPAN: | 100-110 cm. (38-44 in.) |
| MASS: | male average 315 gm. (11 oz.); |
| | female average 380 gm. (13.5 oz.) |
| TERRITORY: | highly variable >.03km$^2$ |
| CLUTCH: | 4-14 |
| EGGS: | white; eliptical to oval; |
| | ~39 x 31 mm. (1.5 x 1.2 in.) |
| INCUBATION: | 21-23 days |
| FLEDGING: | 31-36 days |

The Short-eared Owl is a pale prairie and grassland dweller. It is the most diurnal of the medium-sized owls. Although very often active in broad daylight, it prefers a more crepuscular lifestyle than a fully diurnal one. Groups of these owls will often roost together on the ground or in trees near wetlands on wintering grounds. Hunting is accomplished from an elevated perch such as a fence post, or on the wing, cruising, circling and hovering. It will dive abruptly at spotted prey. Because of their ground-nesting habits, Short-eared Owl eggs and young are particularly vulnerable to predation.

The Short-eared Owl lacks long ear tufts but does at times display short "horns". Raw sienna, raw umber and white are the dominant colors in the short-eared's plumage. Its eyes are yellow, surrounded by a ring of dark plumage and its bill is essentially black. The crown, nape, throat and belly are boldly streaked. Scapulars, cape, back, rump and wing coverts are spotted, while flight feathers and tail are barred.

**OTHER ENGLISH NAMES**
Prairie owl; marsh owl; bog owl

**DIMORPHISM**
On average, females are larger than males.

**DISTRIBUTION**
This owl is found in all continents except Australia. In North America, the Short-eared Owl breeds from arctic Alaska, Yukon and the Northwest Territories to northern Quebec, Labrador and Newfoundland, south to the Canadian maritimes and Great Lakes region in the east through central midwestern United States to Montana and Washington and south through the western states as far as California. It winters in the southern United States and Mexico.

**HABITAT**
The Short-eared Owl breeds over a wide range of habitats including arctic and subarctic environments, boreal, coniferous and some mixed forests and grasslands. Typically, it lives near meadows, marshes, swamps and bogs.

**SUBSPECIES**
Up to ten subspecies of Short-eared Owls are recognized worldwide; however North America has only one race -

*Asio flammeus flammeus.*

**VOICE**
Less vociferous than most owls, the Short-eared Owl utters only one commonly heard call. This territorial and courtship song consists of a string of 16 to 20 low-pitched hoots.." poo-poo-poo-poo-poo..." In addition to this, a snarly "kreee-yow" is uttered by both male and female in recognition. Other calls include various whistles, barks and yelps.

**BREEDING HABITS**
Nest sites of the Short-eared Owl are almost invariably chosen on the ground under the protection of vegetation. A shallow, rudimentary nest is typically scoured into well-drained soil. The nest is usually lined with grass and other soft vegetation. Up to 14 eggs are laid, but a more common clutch size is 5 or 6. The female incubates for 21 to 23 days while the male hunts and provides food. Chicks fledge after 31 to 26 days.

**MIGRATION**
The Short-eared Owl is highly migratory (see distribution) and its presence on numerous oceanic islands attests to its nomadic tendencies. Birds breeding in temperate climates may remain residents year-round provided

food is plentiful, but migrations occur east-west almost as commonly as north-south. Large groups of these birds may appear suddenly in areas of small mammal population explosions.

**PREY**
Small mammals are the dietary staple; however, the Short-eared Owl regularly feeds on a variety of insects and at least 60 species of passerines, waders, seabirds and shorebirds. Regular mammalian prey include mice, shrews, voles, lemmings, pocket gophers, rabbits, weasels and bats. Large insects, such as orthopterans and lepidopterans and coleopterans represent most of their insect prey.

JW '97
½ SIZE
SHORT-EARED OWL

# Short-eared Owl

Scale: 44%

# Boreal Owl

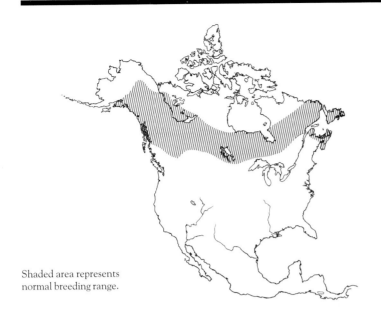

Shaded area represents normal breeding range.

| STATISTICS | |
|---|---|
| STATUS: | uncommon |
| LENGTH: | 22-30 cm. (8.5-12 in) |
| WINGSPAN: | 48-63 cm. (19-25 in ) |
| MASS: | male average 100 gm. (3.5 oz.); |
| | female average 140 gm. (5 oz.) |
| LIFESPAN: | 16 years |
| CLUTCH: | 3-10 |
| EGGS: | white; ~32 x 27 mm. |
| | ( 1.2 x 1.1 in. ) |
| INCUBATION: | 27-28 days |
| FLEDGING: | 28-33 days |

With the exception of individuals in the northernmost part of its range, the Boreal Owl is a strictly nocturnal species. Northern birds are active in daylight when night vanishes during the summer. During the winter months, Boreal Owls will often cache food in tree cavities for future consumption. The Boreal Owl is very similar in appearance and structure to the Saw-whet Owl, but larger and darker, mostly umber and lacking the rusty coloration. Its plumage is thicker and softer than the Saw-whet's as is typical of boreal species. Its legs, tarsi and toes are also heavily feathered. As with the Saw-whet, the flight feathers and tail are not barred , but are sparsely marked with spots at feather edges, where one might suppose bars would be.

## OTHER ENGLISH NAMES
Tengmalm's Owl; Richardson's Owl; sparrow owl

## DIMORPHISM
Females are significantly larger than males.

## DISTRIBUTION
Holarctic. Boreal Owls nest, as far north as northern Alaska, the Yukon, and northern regions of central Canadian provinces to Quebec and Labrador. They breed south through Montana, Wyoming, Colorado, to just north of the United States/Mexico border. East of the Rockies, it will breed as far south as the northern States and the Canadian maritime provinces.

## HABITAT
Coniferous and mixed forests in northern North America are home to the Boreal Owl, specifically boreal and coniferous mountain environments. Trees characteristically abundant in their habitat include spruce, poplar, birch, pine, fir, willow and alder. It may reside up to 3300 m., in the Rocky Mountains. Usually proximate to bogs and marshes.

## SUBSPECIES
Although as many as five races of Boreal Owls are recognized in the world, there is only one representative in North America - Aegolius funereus richardsoni.

## VOICE
The Boreal Owl is capable of at least a dozen calls. Its most common, territorial call consists of a long series of staccato notes in clusters of 5 or 6... "Hoop-poop-poop-poop-poop... hoop-poop..."

## BREEDING HABITS
The most common nest sites are vacant woodpecker holes, usually those of Pileated Woodpeckers. Natural tree cavities are only occasionally used while abandoned open nests are rarely chosen. The male provides the incubating female with food. Clutch size, highly dependent on the availability of food, can be as high as 10 eggs. Normally, though, 3 to 5 eggs are laid per nesting. Incubation usually lasts 27 or 28 days and young fledge 28 to 33 days after hatching.

## MIGRATION
They are generally considered resident; however they may at times migrate to better hunting grounds.

## PREY
Voles, mice and shrews compose the majority of the Boreal Owl's diet. Lemmings, squirrels and other small rodents are also regularly taken. Birds form a small part of their diet (only when mammals are unavailable) and insects, an even smaller part.

JW '97
FULL-SIZE
BOREAL OWL

135

# Boreal Owl

**Scale: 82%**

# Northern Saw-whet Owl

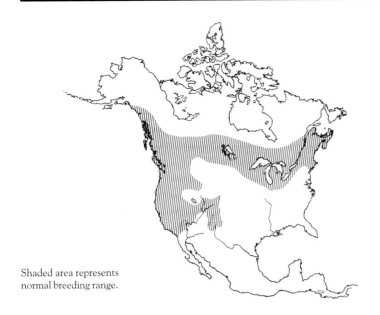

Shaded area represents
normal breeding range.

**STATISTICS**

| | |
|---|---|
| STATUS: | locally common |
| LENGTH: | 17.8-21 cm. (7-8.5 in.) |
| WINGSPAN: | 43-51cm. (17-20 in.) |
| MASS: | 90 gm. (3 oz.) |
| LIFESPAN: | 17 years (in captivity) |
| CLUTCH: | 4-7 |
| EGGS: | white; ~30 x 25 mm. (1.2 x 1 in.) |
| INCUBATION: | 26-28 days |
| FLEDGING: | 27-34 days |

The Saw-whet Owl is the smallest of the hornless owls in eastern North America. The large eyes, friendly expression, extreme tameness and proximity to civilization make the Saw-whet the most popular owl among the general public, who often mistake such a visitor as a "baby" owl. Contrary to popular belief, the name "Saw-whet" is almost certainly not derived from an allusion to a call made by the owl. The roots of this English name are likely from the desecration of the old French Canadian term for the species..."chouette".

The Saw-whet is a white and sienna to umber mix, with feather centres streaked with sienna on its side, chest and belly over a soft white background. Its upper parts are a darker sienna to umber. Its crown is streaked and spotted in white, continuing in a vague "V" around to the back side of the head. Nape, cape, scapular, back and rump feather tracts are only sparsely marked in white, if at all. The outermost feathers on the scapulars are boldly marked with large white markings. Eyes are yellow to orange-yellow, surrounded by dark patches of feathers of variable shapes. Structurally, the Saw-whet Owl differs very little from the Boreal Owl. Toes are only sparsely feathered.

## OTHER ENGLISH NAMES
Kirtland's owl; acadian owl; saw-filer; whetsaw; white-fronted owl; sparrow owl.

## DIMORPHISM
Females are only slightly larger than males on average.

## DISTRIBUTION
Saw-whets breed continuously from the Pacific coast in southwestern Alaska, south through the mountainous western interior to northern Mexico, across southern Canada and the northern states to the Atlantic coast in Nova Scotia.

## HABITAT
The Saw-whet Owl dwells in a wide range of habitats including southern boreal forests, tamarack bogs, mountain slopes, swamps, northern coniferous and mixed forests, clearings and grasslands, and aspen and willow thickets, usually close to water. It can be found living up to 2800 m (9000 ft) above sea level.

## SUBSPECIES
Little variation exists over the Saw-whet Owl's range although the dark coloured birds inhabiting the Queen Charlotte Islands are recognized as *Aegolius acadicus brooksi*.

## VOICE
The territorial call is a long series of evenly-spaced monotonous notes... too-too-too-too... There are also wails, whistles and screeches.

## BREEDING HABITS
Nest sites are usually chosen close to water in a vacant woodpecker hole or natural tree cavity. Incubation is performed by the female, while the male supplies her with food. As many as seven eggs will be laid per nesting; however, the usual clutch size is 5 to 6 eggs. Incubation lasts 26 to 28 days. Young fledge in 27 to 34 days.

## MIGRATION
Northern populations migrate south.

## PREY
Small rodents, including mice, voles, shrews, rats, squirrels and bats, form the majority of the Saw-whet Owl's diet. The owls also rely on a wide variety of songbirds and rarely large insects.

JW '97
Full-sized
Northern Saw-whet Owl

# Northern Saw-whet Owl

Scale: 100%

# Jeff's Painting Notes

## BARN OWL

**Upperparts:** Values of Raw Sienna ,small amounts of Burnt Sienna and Titanium White with small dark spots (Burnt Umber and Raw Umber) and greyish vermiculations (Burnt Umber, Raw Umber and Titanium White.
**Underparts:** Titanium White with some Raw Sienna.
**Toepads:** Burnt Sienna and Titanium White.
**Bill:** Titanium White with Burnt Sienna and Raw Sienna.
**Eyes:** 15mm; Yellow Light.

## FLAMMULATED OWL

**Upperparts:** Mottled dark and light values of Burnt Umber, Raw Umber, Carbon Black and Titanium White. Rusty color on scapulars Burnt Sienna and Raw Sienna.
**Underparts:** Same as Upperparts interspersed with same rusty color.
**Toepads:** Titanium White with Raw Sienna and Carbon Black.
**Bill:** Titanium White with Carbon Black and Raw Sienna.
**Eyes:** 11mm; Burnt Umber and Raw Umber.

## EASTERN SCREECH OWL

*RED PHASE*
**Upperparts:** Subtly darker and lighter values of Burnt Sienna, Raw Sienna and Titanium White. Dark markings Burnt Umber and Raw Umber.
**Underparts:** Same as upperparts. Legs and tarsi Titanium White with Raw Sienna and Burnt Sienna.
**Toepads:** Titanium White with Burnt Sienna and some Raw Sienna.
**Bill:** Titanium White with Carbon Black and Raw Sienna.
**Eyes:** 14-15mm; Yellow Light.

*GREY PHASE*
See Western Screech Owl

## WESTERN SCREECH OWL

**Upperparts:** Dark markings Raw Umber and Raw Sienna with some Carbon Black. Light mottling, Titanium White tinted with dark mix.
**Underparts:** Same as upperparts. Legs and tarsi Titanium White with Raw Sienna and Burnt Sienna.
**Toepads:** Titanium White with Burnt Sienna and some Yellow Ochre.
**Bill:** Titanium White with Carbon Black and Raw Sienna.
**Eyes:** 14-15mm; Yellow Light.

## WHISKERED OWL

**Upperparts:** Dark markings Burnt Umber, Carbon Black and Raw Sienna. Light markings Titanium White tinted with dark mix.
**Underparts:** Same as upperparts. Legs and tarsi with Titanium White with Raw Sienna and Burnt Sienna.
**Toepads:** Titanium White with Carbon Black and Yellow Ochre.
**Bill:** Titanium White with Carbon Black and Raw Sienna.
**Eyes:** 13mm; Yellow Light .

## GREAT HORNED OWL

**Upperparts:** Raw Umber and Burnt Umber for dark markings. Titanium White with dark mix for light areas. Rusty areas of Raw Sienna and Burnt Sienna.
**Underparts:** Same as upperparts.
**Toepads:** Raw Sienna, Titanium White and some Burnt Sienna.
**Bill:** Carbon Black, Burnt Umber and Raw Umber
**Eyes:** 20mm; Yellow Light.

## SNOWY OWL

**Upperparts:** Titanium White tinted with dark mix and Yellow Ochre.
**Underparts:** Same as upperparts.
**Toepads:** Raw Sienna, Titanium White and some Burnt Sienna.
**Bill:** Carbon Black, Burnt Umber and Raw Umber.
**Eyes:** 20mm; Yellow Light.

## NORTHERN HAWK OWL

**Upperparts:** Dark areas, Raw Umber with small amount of Burnt Umber. Light markings, Titanium White tinted with dark mix.
**Underparts:** Same as upperparts plus some Burnt Sienna and Raw Sienna in rear dark markings.
**Toepads:** Raw Sienna, Titanium White and some Burnt Sienna.
**Bill:** Raw Sienna, Yellow Ochre and Titanium White.
**Eyes:** 14-15mm; Yellow Light.

## NORTHERN PYGMY OWL

**Upperparts:** Dark areas Raw Umber and Burnt Umber and Raw Sienna wtih Titanium White markings, tinted with dark mix.
**Underparts:** Dark markings darker than upperparts (with Carbon Black).
**Toepads:** Raw Sienna, Burnt Sienna, Titanium White.
**Bill:** Raw Sienna, Yellow Ochre and Titanium White.
**Eyes:** 7-8mm; Yellow Light.

## FERRUGINOUS PYGMY OWL

**Upperparts:** Dark areas Burnt Umber with Burnt Sienna. Light areas, tinted

Titanium White.
**Underparts**: Dark markings darker than upperparts (with Carbon Black).
**Toepads**: Raw Sienna, Burnt Sienna, Titanium White.
**Bill**: Raw Sienna, Yellow Ochre and Titanium White.
**Eyes**: 7-8mm; Yellow Light.

## ELF OWL

**Upperparts**: Raw Umber, Burnt Umber, Raw Sienna and Burnt Sienna mottled with Titanium White.
**Underparts**: Same as upperparts.
**Toepads**: Raw Sienna, Raw Umber and White.
**Bill**: Carbon Black, Titanium White, and Raw Sienna.
**Eyes**: 6-7mm; Yellow Light.

## BURRROWING OWL

**Upperparts**: Raw Sienna with Titanium White and Burnt Sienna. Darkest areas Raw Umber and Burnt Umber.
**Underparts**: Same as upperparts.
**Toepads**: Raw Umber with Titanium White and Burnt Sienna.
**Bill**: Raw Umber, Raw Sienna and Titanium White.
**Eyes**: 13mm; Yellow Light.

## BARRED OWL

**Upperparts**: Raw Umber and Burnt Umber with Burnt Sienna. Light markings, Titanium White tinted with dark mix.
**Underparts**: Same as upperparts, but lighter areas tinted with Raw Sienna and Yellow Ochre.
**Toepads**: Raw Sienna, Burnt Umber and Titanium White
**Bill**: Yellow Ochre, Raw Sienna, Titanium White.
**Eyes**: 20mm; Burnt Umber and Raw Umber.

## SPOTTED OWL

**Upperparts**: Raw Umber and Burnt Umber with Burnt Sienna. Light markings, Titanium White tinted with dark mix.
**Underparts**: Same as upperparts, but lighter areas tinted with Raw Sienna, Burnt Sienna and Yellow Ochre.
**Toepads**: Raw Sienna, Burnt Umber and Titanium White
**Bill**: Yellow Ochre, Raw Sienna, Titanium White.
**Eyes**: 20mm; Burnt Umber and Raw Umber.

## GREAT GRAY OWL

**Upperparts**: Dark values, Raw umber slightly lightened with Titanium White. Light markings, the reverse.

**Underparts**: Same as upperparts.
**Toepads**: Raw Umber, Raw Sienna and Titanium White.
**Bill**: Raw Sienna, Titanium White, Yellow Ochre and touch of Carbon Black.
**Eyes**: 18-20mm; Yellow Light.

## LONG-EARED OWL

**Upperparts**: Dark areas, Raw Umber and Burnt Umber, with light markings (Titanium White tinted with dark mix) and areas of Raw Sienna and Burnt Sienna.
**Underparts**: Same as upperparts.
**Toepads**: Raw Umber, Raw Sienna and Titanium White.
**Bill**: Carbon Black and Raw Umber
**Eyes**: 14-15mm; Yellow Light

## SHORT-EARED OWL

**Upperparts**: Raw Sienna with some Titanium White and even less Burnt Sienna. Dark markings, Raw Umber with touch of carbon Black and Burnt Umber.
**Underparts**: Same as upperparts.
**Toepads**: Raw Umber, Raw Sienna and Titanium White.
**Bill**: Carbon Black and Raw Umber
**Eyes**: 14-15mm; Yellow Light

## BOREAL OWL

**Upperparts:** Dark and light values of Raw Umber with a small amount of Burnt Umber.
**Underparts:** Markings same as upperparts. Light areas, Titanium White tinted with upperpart basecolor. Feet and Legs light value with Raw Sienna and small amount of Yellow Ochre.
**Toepads:** Titanium White and Raw Sienna with small amount of Yellow Ochre.
**Bill:** Titanium White, Raw Sienna and Yellow Ochre tinted with upperpart dark mix with Ultramarine Blue.
**Eyes:** 15mm; Yellow Light.

## SAW-WHET OWL

**Upperparts:** Burnt Sienna and Raw Sienna darkened with Carbon Black and washes of Raw Umber and Burnt Umber. Feather edges highlighted with Burnt Sienna/Raw Sienna with Titanium White.
**Underparts:** Markings Burnt Sienna and Raw Sienna darkened with Burnt Umber and Raw umber. Light areas tinted with dark mixture and small amount of Yellow Ochre.
**Toepads:** Burnt Sienna and Titanium White
**Bill:** Burnt umber and Ultramarine Blue.
**Eyes:** 13 mm; Yellow Light with touch of red or orange.

**"Middle of Winter" - Snowy Owl**
© 1995 by Jeremy Pearse
(29"x43")
oil on canvas
private collection

# Glossary

**alula**: a type of retractable flight feather anchored to the hand or "thumb" of birds.

**arachnid**: an animal belonging to the class arachnida, which includes spiders and scorpions

**arthropod**: an animal belonging to the phylum arthropoda, which includes insects and arachnids.

**barb**: the numerous, parallel extensions off the sides of the rachis.

**barbule**: see hammuli

**Coleoptera**: an order of insects which includes beetles.

**crepuscular**: active primarily during dusk.

**cryptic**: camouflaged appearance.

**diurnal**: active primarily during the day.

**fledging time**: the time taken from hatching to leaving the nest.

**Holarctic**: inhabiting the northern hemisphere.

**hammuli**: tiny, parallel barbed extensions which lock the feather barbs together.

**Lepidoptera**: an order of insects which includes moths and butterflies.

**morph**: a color phase or plumage type. ex. The Eastern Screech Owl has two color morphs: red phase and grey phase.

**nocturnal**: active primarily during the night.

**Orthoptera**: an order of insects which includes grasshoppers, crickets, katydids, mole crickets, etc.

**passerines**: perching birds.

**pellet**: an elongated ball of indigestible material regurgitated by certain birds, such as owls, herons and raptors.

**primaries**: outermost flight feathers of birds, which are attached to the metacarpal. Owls have ten primaries.

**rachis**: The central strong shaft of a feather.

**rectrices**: The long tail feathers of birds. All North American owls have 12 rectrices except the Elf Owl, which has 10.

**secondaries**: flight feathers of birds, which are attached to the humerus.

**sedentary**: Birds said to be sedentary reside close to one area year round.

**sexual dimorphism**: differences in appearance between the male of a species and the female of a species. Female owls tend to be significantly larger than males.

**Strigidae**: one of two living families of owls which includes the so-called true owls.

**Strigiformes**: The order of birds which includes all species of owls.

**taiga**: the northern boreal forest biome.

**tapetum lucidum**: an image enhancing adaptation present in many nocturnal animals whereby light is reflected by the tapetum, back across the retina, to increase overall light reception.

**tertials**: flight feathers of birds, which are attached to the humerus.

**Tytonidae**: one of two living families of owls which includes the so-called Monkey-faced Owls. The Barn Owl is the only representative of this family in North America.

**ventriculus**: the glandular sac in the digestive system in which digestible parts of prey are liquified and separated from the remaining undigestible portion (usually including bones, fur and insect casings).

**visual purple**: the chemical, rhodopsin found in the rod cells of owls which enhances light images.

# Recommended Reading

American Ornithologists' Union, 1983. *Checklist of North American Birds*. 6th ed. Baltimore.

Audubon, J.J. 1870. *Birds of America*. Vols 1and 2. New York: George R. Lockwood.

Burton, J.A., ed. 1984. *Owls of the World: Their Evolution, Structure and Ecology*. 2nd ed. Dover, New Hampshire: Tanager Books.

Clark, R.J., D.G. Smith, and L.H. Kelso. 1978. *Working Bibliography of Owls of the World*. Washington, D.C.: National Wildlife Federation.

DeBenedictis, Paul A. 1992. Birds of the world. *Birding* 24, 3, pp. 188-194.

de la Torre, J. 1990. *Owls: Their Life and Behavior*. New York, New York: Crown Publishers.

Ehrlich, P.R., D.S. Dobkin, and D. Wheye. 1988. *The Birder's Handbook: A Field Guide to the Natural History of North American Birds*. New York: Simon and Schuster.

Everett, M. 1977. *A Natural History of Owls*. London: Hamlyn.

Farrand, J., Jr. ed. 1983. *The Audubon Society Master Guide to Birding*. Vol. 2. New York: Knopf.

Godfrey, W. E. 1979. *The Birds of Canada*. Ottawa: National Museums of Canada.

Harrison, H.H. 1975. *A Field Guide to Birds' Nests*. Boston: Houghton Mifflin.

Hume, R. 1991. *Owls of the World*. Philadelphia: Running Press.

Johnsgard, P.A. 1988. *North American Owls*. Washington: Smithsonian Institution Press.

Lucas, Alfred M. and Peter R. Stettenheim. 1972. *Avian Integument, Part I*, Agricultural Handbook 362. Washington, D.C.: United States Department of Agriculture.

McKeever, K. 1979. *Care and Rehabilitation of Injured Owls*. Rannie, Ontario: The Owl Rehabilitation Research Foundation.

Mikkola, H. 1983. *Owls of Europe*. Vermillion, S.D.: Buteo Books.

Monroe, Burt L., Jr. and Charles G. Sibley. 1993. *A World Checklist of Birds*. NewHaven and London: Yale University Press.

Mowat, F. 1961. *Owls in the Family*. Boston: Little, Brown.

Nero, R.W. 1980. *The Great Gray Owl, Phantom of the Northern Forest*. Washington, D.C.: Smithsonian Institution Press.

Peterson, R.T. 1980. *A Field Guide to the Birds*. Boston: Houghton Mifflin.

Runtz, Michael. 1996. *Wild Wings*, The Hidden World of Birds. Erin, Ontario: Boston Mills Press.

Sibley, Charles G. and Burt L. Munroe, Jr.. 1990. *Distribution and Taxonomy of Birds of the World*. New Haven and London: Yale University Press.

Sibley, Charles G. and Burt L. Monroe, Jr. 1993. *Supplement to Distribution and Taxonomy of Birds of the World*. New Haven and London: Yale University Press.

Sibley, Charles G., Jon E. Ahlquist and Burt L. Monroe, Jr. 1988. A classification of the living birds of the world based on DNA-DNA hybridization studies, *Auk 105*, 1988, pp. 409-423..

Sibley, Charles G. and Jon E. Ahlquist. 1990. *Phylogeny and Classification of Birds: A Study in Molecular Evolution*. New Haven and London: Yale University Press.

Snetsinger, Phoebe B., Pete Whan and Simon Harrap. 1992. The New Taxonomy: Three Perspectives, *Birding* 24, 6, pp. 381-387.

Sparks, John and Tony Soper. 1989. *Owls* - 2nd ed. Great Britain: David and Charles Publishers.

Sutton, P. and C. Sutton. 1994. *How to Spot Owls*. Shelburne, Vermont: Chapters Publishing.

Taylor, Ian. 1994. *Barn Owls: predator- prey relationships and conservation*. Great Britain: Cambridge University Press.

Terres, J.K. 1980. *Audubon Society Encyclopedia of North American Birds*. New York: Knopf.

Toops, Connie. 1990. *Discovering Owls*. North Vancouver: Whitecap Books.

Voous, Karel. H. 1989. *Owls of the Northern Hemisphere*. Cambridge, Massachusetts: MIT Press.

Walker, L.W. 1974. *The Book of Owls*. New York: Knopf.

## Discography

*Voices of New World Nightbirds: Owls, Nightjars and their Allies.* ARA Records, 1986.

*A Field Guide to Bird Songs of Eastern and Central North America.* Cornell Laboratory of Ornithology. (Accompanies Roger Tory Peterson's *Field Guide to the Birds*.)

*A Field Guide to the Songs of Western Birds.* Cornell Laboratory of Ornithology. (Accompanies Roger Tory Peterson's *Field Guide to Western Birds*.)

*Guide to Bird Sounds.* National Geographic Society. (Accompanies the NGS"s *Field Guide to the Birds of North America*.)

**"Screech Owl Pair with Pine Cones"**
**- Western Screech Owl**
© 1992 by Edward Aldrich
(12"x16")
oil on masonite
private collection

# Contributing Artists & Photography Credits

**Allaben-Confer, Karen L.**
U.S.A.
b. 1947
Resides: Brooktondale, NY
Photography by Jon Reis Photography, Ithaca, NY.
Courtesy of Karen Allaben-Confer.

**Aldrich, Edward**
U.S.A.
b. 1965
Resides: Broomfield, CO
Courtesy of Edward Aldrich.

**Allmond, Charles**
U.S.A.
b. 1931
Resides: Wilmington, DE,
Bronzes of "Patience" are available from the artist @ 104 Rowland Park Boulevard, Wilmington, DE, 19803
Courtesy of Charles Allmond.

**Angell, Tony**
U.S.A.
b. 1940
Resides:Seattle, WA
Reproductions of Mr. Angell's work are available c/o Foster/White Gallery, 311¹/₂ Occidental, Seattle, WA, U.S.A. 98155
Courtesy of Tony Angell.

**Arneill, Brian**
U.K.
b. 1953
Resides: Kirkcudbrightshire, Scotland
Courtesy of Brian Arneill.

**Banthien, Barbara**
U.S.A
b. 1950
Resides: Tiberon, CA
Courtesy of Barbara Banthien.

**Barnard, Allan**
Canada
b. 1961
Resides: Hamilton, ON
Photography by See Spot Run, Toronto.
Courtesy of Allan Barnard.

**Cameron, Clarence P.**
U.S.A
b. 1941
Resides: Madison, WI
Courtesy of Clarence Cameron.

**Dumas, Michael**
Canada
b. 1950
Resides: Peterborough, ON
Limited edition prints of "The Last Leaves of Autumn" and "Prairie Cradle" are available from Buckhorn Fine Art Publishing, Box 10, Buckhorn, ON, K0L 1J0, (800) 461-1787 or (705) 657-1107
Courtesy of Buckhorn Fine Art Publishing.

**Dunn, Kathleen E.**
U.S.A.
b. 1955
Resides: Kent, WA
Photography by Richard Nichol.
Courtesy of Kathleen Dunn.

**DuRose, Edward**
U.S.A.
b. 1956
Resides: Roseville, MN
Courtesy of Edward DuRose.

**Eigenberger, Gary J.**
U.S.A.
b. 1960
Resides: Green Bay, WI
Courtesy of Gary Eigenberger.

**Erlund, Beth**
U.S.A.
b. 1947
Resides: Morrison, CO
Reproductions of "Nightwings" and "Do Not Disturb" are available from MT Wilderness Press, 22528 Blue Jay, Morrison, CO, U.S.A. 80465
Courtesy of Beth Erlund.

**Flahey, Barry C.**
Canada
Resides: Manotick, ON
Reproductions of "After the Storm" are available from the artist @ P.O. Box 298, Manotick, ON, Canada, K4M 1A3, (613) 692-1504 or (613) 759-1785
Courtesy of Barry Flahey.

**Frederick, Rod**
U.S.A.
b. 1956
Resides: Bend, OR
Reproductions of all of Mr. Fredrick's work featured in this publication are available from The Greenwich Workshop, One Greenwich Place, Shelton, CT, U.S.A. 06484, (800) 243-4246.
Courtesy of The Greenwich Workshop.

**Hunkel, Cary**
U.S.A.
b. 1945
Resides: Madison, WI
Courtesy of Cary Hunkel.

**Hutchinson, Andrew**
U.K.
b. 1961
Resides: Morayshire, Scotland
Reproductions of "Barn Owl" are available from Waxwing Fine Arts, 36A High Street, Grantown-on-Spey, Morayshire, PH263EH, Scotland, U.K., 01479 873513
Photography by Alan Hampson.
Courtesy of Andrew Hutchinson.

**Isaac, Terry**
U.S.A.
b. 1958
Resides: Salem, OR
Signed and numbered limited edition prints by Terry Isaac are available through Mill Pond Press, Inc.., 310 Center Court, Venice, FL 34292
Courtesy of the Mill Pond Press, Inc.

**Johnson, David B.**
Canada
b. 1947
Resides: Nepean, ON
"Saw-whet Owl" photography by Ray Pilon
"Snowy Owl" courtesy of Lee Valley Tools

**Kanouse, M.C.**
U.S.A.
b. 1936
Resides: Grand Rapids, MI
Courtesy of M.C. Kanouse.

**Klafke, Michael A.**
U.S.A.
b. 1953
Resides: Onalaska, WI
Photography by Imageworks Inc., Lacrosse, WI
Courtesy of Michael Klafke.

**Karstad, Aleta**
Canada
b. 1951
Resides: Bishops Mills, ON
Photography by Ernie Sparks, Kingston, ON.

**Lyman, Stephen**
U.S.A.
b. 1957
Resides: Sandpoint, ID
Courtesy of The Greenwich Workshop, Shelton, CT.

**Markowski, Cindy**
U.S.A.
b. 1943
Resides: Wausau, WI

Courtesy of Cindy Markowski.

**Matia, Walt**
U.S.A.
b. 1953
Resides: Poolesville, MD
Bronzes of "Nobody's Angel" are available from Curlew Castings, 18601 Darnestown Rd., Poolesville MD., 20837.
Photography by Mark Gulezian.
Courtesy of Walt Matia.

**Nogy, Arnold**
Canada
b. 1965
Resides: Coldwater, ON
Limited edition prints of "Narrow Escape" and "The Noble" are available from the artist @ RR 2, Coldwater, ON, Canada, L0K 1E0, (705) 835-2703
Photography by Paul Miszczyk.
Courtesy of Arnold Nogy.

**Paul, Dr. Jeremy**
U.K.
b. 1954
Resides: Isle of Man, U.K.
Reproductions of "Uncertain Outlook" are available from J. Paul Publishing, 4 Ballachrink, Colby, Isle of Man, U.K. 1M9 4PB. Tel 44 1624 832980
Photography by T. Lakin.
Courtesy of Dr. Jeremy Paul.

**Pearse, Jeremy**
U.S.A.
b. 1959
Resides: Gaithersburg, MD
Courtesy of Jeremy Pearse.

**Pitcher, John Charles**
U.S.A.
b. 1949
Resides: Dorset, VT
Courtesy of John Pitcher.

**Rich, Andrea**
U.S.A.
b. 1954
Resides: Santa Cruz, CA
Woodcuts of "Burrowing Owls" are available from the artist @ 706 Western Drive, Santa Cruz, CA 95060 (408)429-6790
Courtesy of Andrea Rich.

**Ross, Suellen**
U.S.A.
b. 1941
Resides: Seattle, WA
Courtesy of Suellen Ross.

**Sharrock, Joan**
Canada
b. 1946
Resides: Vancouver, BC
Photography by Gamma Pro Lab, Vancouver, BC.
Courtesy of Joan Sharrock.

**Sill, John**
U.S.A.
b. 1947
Resides: Franklin, NC
Courtesy of John Sill.

**Soulliere, John**
U.S.A.
b. 1941
Resides: Marietta, GA.
Courtesy of John Soulliere.

**Uchiyama, Haruo**
Japan
b. 1950
Resides: Chiba, Japan
Courtesy of Haruo Uchiyama.

**van Frankenhuyzen, Gijsbert**
U.S.A.
b. 1951
Resides: Bath, MI
Photography by Dembinski Photo Assoc.
Courtesy of Gijsbert van Frankenhuyzen.

**Waterman, Paula**
U.S.A.
b. 1954
Resides: Annapolis, MD
Photography by Martin and Bond Photography, Annapolis, MD.
Courtesy of Paula Waterman

**Whiting, Jeffrey**
Canada
b. 1972
Resides: Clayton, ON
Photography by Ernie Sparks, Kingston, ON

All photography of Illustrations in *Species Profiles* section by Ernie Sparks, Kingston, ON

Versals appearing in *Foreword, Introduction* and *Owls at a Glance* sections were created specifically for this book by Aleta Karstad and are copyrighted.

Overleaf:

**"Short-eared Owl"**
© 1993 by Andrew Hutchinson
(14.5"x20.5")
gouache on Frisk CS2 hot press watercolor board
*private collection

# Colophon

Series and book design and layout by Jeffrey Whiting
Typeset in Goudy Old Style and Dauphin.
Color separations and printing by Gilmore Print Services, Inc.,
Ottawa, Ontario
The text paper, Jenson Gloss 80M
The dust jacket paper, Supreme Gloss 115M
Published by The Heliconia Press, Inc.